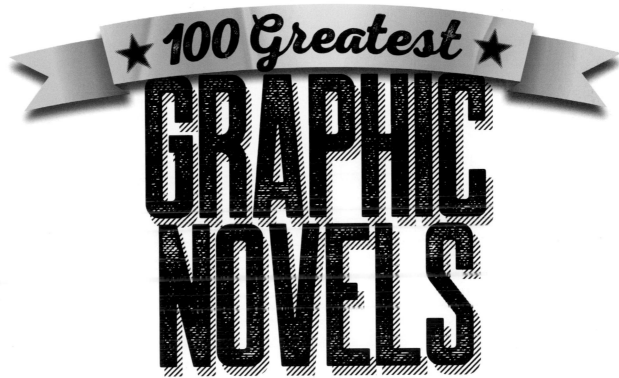

★ 100 Greatest ★
GRAPHIC NOVELS

THE GOOD. THE BAD. THE EPIC.

Katrina Hill AND Alex Langley

Published by

Krause Publications, a division of F+W Media, Inc.
700 East State Street • Iola, WI 54990-0001
715-445-2214 • 888-457-2873
www.krausebooks.com

To order books or other products call toll-free 1-800-258-0929
or visit us online at www.krausebooks.com

Copyright credits for the graphic novels reviewed in this book were taken, when possible, from the copyright information that appears on the material as it originally appeared. When it was not possible, copyright information was culled from reference materials. In no case does Krause Publications/F+W Media, Inc., claim ownership of the copyright to the material shown in the book. Credits are on P. 232.

Unless otherwise noted, photos were provided by the authors.

ISBN-13: 978-1-4402-4710-1
ISBN-10: 1-4402-4710-2

Cover Design by Dave Hauser
Designed by Jana Tappa
Edited by Kristine Manty

Printed in China

10 9 8 7 6 5 4 3 2 1

DEDICATED TO ANYONE WHO HAS
EVER TRIED TO INSPIRE OTHERS
WITH THEIR COMICS,
NOW AND FOREVER.

SPECIAL THANKS

From both:

Thanks to our editor, Kris Manty, and editorial diector, Paul Kennedy, who believed in us from the beginning.

Enormous thanks to Sam Cumings, whose epic collection of graphic novels gave us a ton of great materials and recommendations to work with, and thanks to Marko Head for lending us select items from his collection as well.

From Katrina:

First, and foremost, thanks to Alex for co-authoring this book with me. I couldn't have done this as well (or with my sanity as intact) without him.

I'd also like to thank my siblings from other parents—Renee, Marko, and Nicholas, for just being cool people I could bounce ideas off of or rant to.

Thank you Amy, Debbie, Jennifer, and Tiffany, for many outings of mani/pedis and cocktails to help me unwind after long days of stressful writing.

Thanks to Jane Espenson, Felicia Day, Amy Poehler, Nate Powell, and Raina Telgemeier for inspiring my creative powers with powers of their own.

And, of course, huge thanks to my family for the continued encouragement.

From Alex:

As always, thanks to Katrina, for lots and lots and lots of stuff.

Thanks to Nicholas, Mom, and Dad for being awesome and helping me grow up in an awesome-rich environment.

Thanks to my extended family for encouraging me to do what I do even if you don't always understand what I do.

Thanks to my friends, my second family, who've helped keep me laughing and keep me going. Give yourselves a pat on the back and a tweak of the tushy for me.

Thanks to the Denton Writer's Critique Group for putting up with my shenanigans as I try to better myself as a professional word-maker and keyboard smasher.

Thanks to the OC Remix community for giving me such amazing music to listen to while working on my many, many projects.

Thanks to the following guys who have inspired me to try to write, think, and be funny since a young age: Bill Murray, "Weird" Al Yankovic, Gary Larson, Bill Watterson, and Terry Pratchett.

CONTENTS

Graphic Novels: The Artistry and the Awesomestry

The entire comics industry is built on a falsehood.

Comic books are named for comedy, so comics are supposed to be funny. Except any comic book fan will tell you that's not always true. Some comics are funny, sure, but plenty others aren't supposed to be.

Plenty of comic books are ornately built and thought-provoking, bearing striking visuals and masterful layouts working in tandem with dialogue and description to create a whole that's stronger than the sum of its parts. Through this medium, audiences have received some of the most intelligent, mature stories created in the last century, all because the art form of comics has evolved well beyond its name, and the most developed form of this evolution comes bearing a new, more appropriate title: graphic novels.

Graphic novels can take us to fantastic, yet human worlds with stories like *The Arrival,* show us the darkest parts of history with tales like the Pulitzer Prize-winning *Maus,* tickle our funny bones with goofballs like *Scott Pilgrim,* or take us on superheroic adventures with characters like the *Guardians of the Galaxy*. Graphic novels cover any and all topics, and, to put it scientifically, they're freaking awesome. But, still, one question lingers in the mind of the literature-minded public: what, exactly, *is* a graphic novel?

"Does a picture book count as a graphic novel," you ask? Perhaps, depending on how many pictures are there and how the words are arranged. "Does a collection of comic book issues qualify?" Possibly, depending on the story. "What about my four-hundred-page fan comic about Sonic the Hedgehog's love quadrangle with EVA from *Wall-E* and the Starbucks from both versions of *Battlestar Galactica*?" Maybe that's a graphic novel, maybe not. We'd have to read it, and we really don't want to.

The point is that, much like the term *comic,* what qualifies as a graphic novel is up for debate. For our purposes, we'll just say a graphic novel is a longform[1] version of a comic book, where images and words unite together in sequence to form a complete story or message. Much like comic books in general, graphic novels have often been thought of as something for kids to read and adults to ignore, despite the fact that, for decades, creators have forged graphic novels which are as mature and insightful as stories from any other medium. Fortunately, now more and more people are starting to recognize this art form for its true, infinite potential, so, whether you're a member of the old guard, the new guard, or the somewhere-in-between guard, come with us for a guided tour through some of the greatest graphic novels the world has to offer.

---

1 How many pages long does it have to be? Let's say 42, give or take a few hundred pages. If it's a good enough number for Douglas Adams, it's good enough for us.

THE GREATEST AT A GLANCE

CHAPTER 1

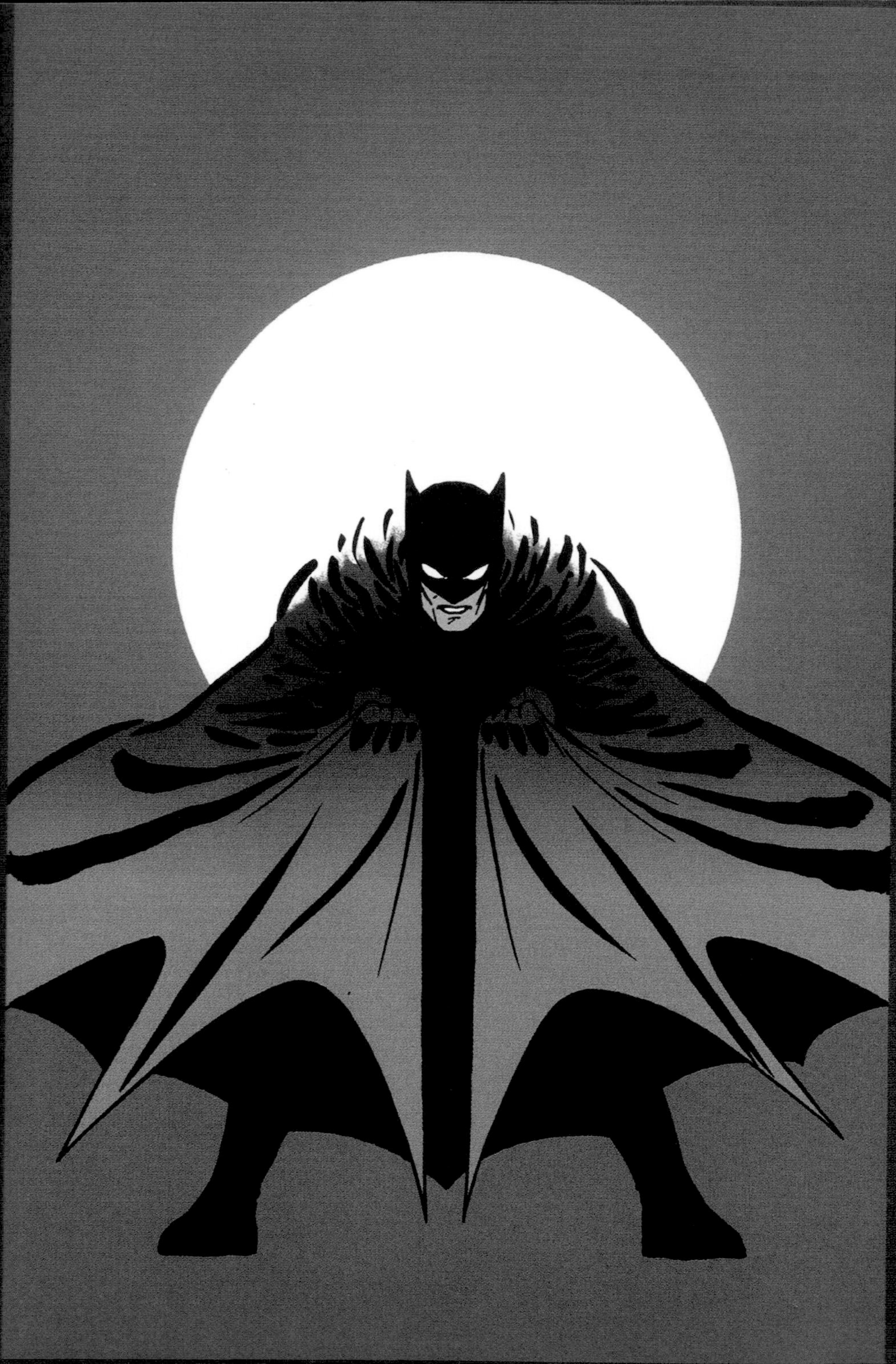

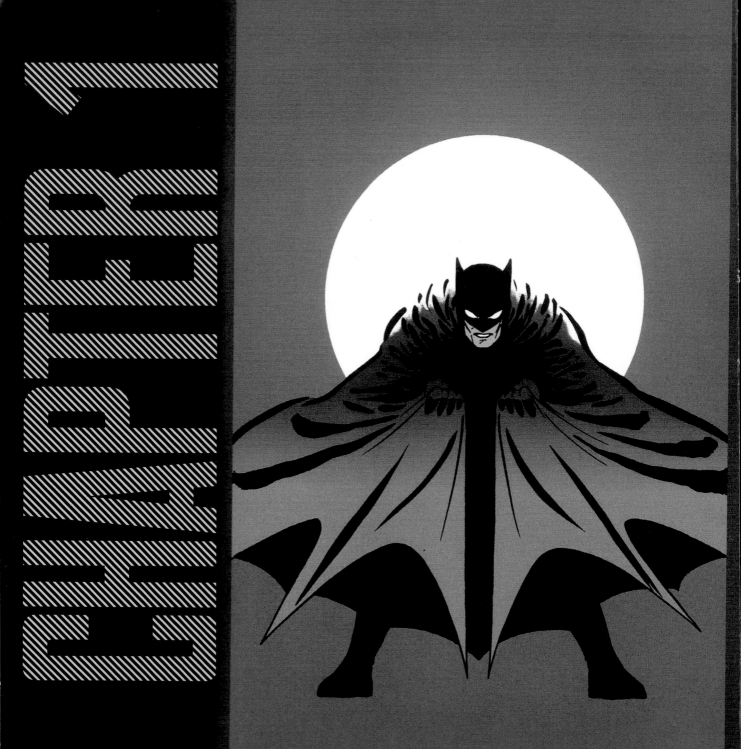

MORE THAN HUMAN:
THE SUPERHEROIC MYTH

////////////////////

Superheroic stories trace their origin back to early human history with the myths of ancient civilization. Greece's Hercules, the Wabanaki's Glooscap, even early American mythic figures like John Henry, Paul Bunyan, and Nicolas Cage serve as the basis for characters we now commonly refer to as "superheroes." These beings are larger-than-life, able to accomplish unbelievable feats through any combination of fate-given abilities and raw determination. Some were believed to be real by their culture while others were only referred to in legend, but through their fictional examples, they helped inspire the spirits and imaginations of the people.

The first modern superhero is Superman, who flew onto the scene in 1938 by body-slamming a runaway car into a rock in *Action Comics #1*[2]. Superman represents the archetypal superhero, with his flowing cape, the bright symbol across his chest, and a selection of superpowers which have all been copied countless times by later writers. After the Man of Steel landed on newsstands, other heroes followed suit. Captain America marked his first arrival by punching Hitler in the face on the cover

of *Captain America Comics #1*[3]. Then came Wonder Woman, a Greek mythology-inspired heroine whose primary tool was a lasso of truth—an unsurprising armament given that Wonder Woman's creator, William Moulton Marston, also helped create the polygraph, the machine commonly known as the lie detector.[4] During these early days of superheroic stories, morality was an uncomplicated affair. Heroes were good, the villains were evil, and after a well-deserved sock to the jaw, all guilty parties were off to jail. Given the tumultuousness of World War II, it's no surprise that such clear-cut tales of heroics appealed to audiences. Even the darkest of these new heroes, Batman, still had bright, cheery adventures with simple resolutions despite the character's unusually tragic origin.[5]

With Batman and, to some extent, Captain America, audiences received stories about the triumph of human will. These were two ordinary men put through extraordinary circumstances to become something incredible. Superman and Wonder Woman, on the other hand, represented more of a superhuman ideal. These were characters whose

---

2 *Action Comics # 1*, Siegel & Schuster, 1938.

3 *Captain America Comics*, Simon & Kirby, 1941.
4 *All-Star Comics #8*, Marston, 1941.
5 *Detective Comics #27*, Finger & Kane, 1939.

origins were extraplanetary or magical in nature, characters we could never be, yet we couldn't help but dream about being. For the duration of what's referred to as the Golden Age of Comics, superhero comics continued this general trend of simplistic, exciting stories. In 1962, however, Stan Lee and Steve Ditko created a character who marked a massive shift in the zeitgeist of the genre. This new character was a superhero, yes, but he wasn't a billionaire like Batman, nor did he come from an otherworldly lineage like Superman or Wonder Woman. He was an ordinary teen trying his best to help out while still dealing with everyday problems. Girls weren't interested in him, the boys were mostly interested in bullying him, and his elderly caretakers were beginning to need more care than they could give him. Spider-Man had a lot of real-world problems to deal with from the get-go, but one problem he didn't have to worry about was whether his comic would continue being published, as *Amazing Fantasy #15*[6] was an immediate hit. The public loved his blend of superheroic action and real-world problems; this marked a shift in storytelling that transformed the industry.[7] Suddenly, more realistic heroes were popping up everywhere, many of whom, like the X-Men, were used as metaphors for real issues such as racism and bigotry. Though superhero stories had tackled such problems before, they'd never done so with such frequency or zeal. The superhero stories of decades before were written, largely, for children. These stories were a bit more mature, matching an

audience that had matured with them.

The genre continued to mature throughout the Silver and Bronze ages of comics and well into the 1980s, where another shift in the zeitgeist transformed superheroes again. An air of uncertain doom permeated much of the 1980s; increasing government power coupled with increasing public distrust, economic instability, and general fears of nuclear war led to a transformation of the pop culture landscape. Movies, television shows, and comic books became darker. Frank Miller's *The Dark Knight Returns* and Alan Moore's *Watchmen*,

---

6 *Amazing Fantasy #15*, Lee & Ditko, 1962.

7 Also marking the beginning of what's referred to as the Silver Age of Comics.

in particular, took the familiar framework of superheroes and applied a grittier, more realistic veneer to it. These complex tales were exactly what the public was in the mood for, and the rest of the comics industry followed suit, thus transitioning into the Modern Age of Comics.

Today, superhero stories, whether on the page or on the screen, are more popular than ever. What is it about these masked heroes which makes them so long-lived? For many, superheroes represent the desire to incite change, the idea that a single person with determination can have a profound effect on the world. Human beings crave importance; our desire for *more* is part of the reason we've evolved our way to the top of the food chain. Through superhero stories, we're able to vicariously live out fantasies of great significance, dreaming about being heroes who stop rampaging supervillains and cosmic threats. Delusions of grandeur and fantasies of adventure aren't the only reason we like superheroes, however. Superheroes, more so than any other genre, present stories of justice, satisfying a craving for a just world that psychologists find to be innate in many people.[8] This *Just World Hypothesis* states that humans believe the world to be a fair place where the good triumph and the bad are punished. Though this subconscious logical fallacy often incites people to blame the unfortunate for their own misfortune, it also leads us to desire stories which confirm this ideal. Lastly, not to get too technical, superheroes are

flat-out cool. They have cool costumes, cool powers, and it's fun to see them take down equally cool (but often less conventionally attractive) bad guys.

---

8 *Lerner*, M. J., & Miller, D. T. (1978). Just world research and the attribution process: Looking back and ahead. Psychological Bulletin, 85(5), 1030–1051.

BATMAN: YEAR ONE

Written by: Frank Miller • Art by: David Mazzucchelli • Publisher: DC Comics; 1987

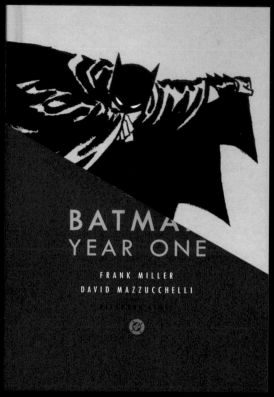

What were the Caped Crusader's early years like? What was it like for the Dark Knight when he was just a Dark Squire? How did Batman begin? *Batman: Year One* answers those questions with a noir-infused story that inspired Christopher Nolan's film trilogy.

Batman: Year One features both Bruce Wayne and Detective Jim Gordon as deuteragonists, each trying to clean up Gotham in their own way. As Batman, Bruce Wayne moves quickly and efficiently through the criminal underworld, taking down the thugs, gangsters, and money-laden criminals preying on his beloved Gotham City, all in the hopes of eliminating the sort of violent crime that cost his parents their lives (and him his childhood). Gordon, on the other hand, has to play by the rules, and as the only honest cop in a hopelessly corrupt police force, his sense of morality puts him into more than a few crosshairs. Both men willingly put themselves in harm's way, never eschewing their valiant ideals out of fear of personal harm. While many tales of vigilante justice paint police as incompetent, Frank Miller chose to depict Gordon as a man of intelligence and principle. Batman serves as a heroic counterpart to him, working in analogue to aid in destroying the corrupt architecture built into Gotham City.

Sharp-eyed readers will note the similarities between David Mazzucchelli's work and Batman's earliest printed issues; Mazzucchelli made a deliberate choice to harken back to those decades-old stories by making use of negative space and implied detail. The muted color palette and watercolor-soaked pages of rain and ruin create an oppressive feeling to Gotham City. In much of Miller's work, he often leans on introspective thoughts, rather than spoken dialogue, to convey his characters, and here is no exception. Since most panels are framed with

Batman finds inspiration from an unlikely beast.

contemplative thought boxes, Mazzucchelli is free to stretch his artistic muscles where needed to create panels filled with heavy, forceful action sequences.

"He's clearly a man with a mission, but it's not one of vengeance. Bruce is not after personal revenge ... He's much bigger than that; he's much more noble than that. He wants the world to be a better place, where a young Bruce Wayne would not be a victim...

"In a way, he's out to make himself unnecessary. Batman is a hero who wishes he didn't have to exist."
—Frank Miller[9]

9 *Batman: Year One*. Frank Miller and David Mazzucchelli.

TRIUMPH AND TORMENT

Written by: Roger Stern • Art by: Mike Mignola and Mark Badger • Publisher: Marvel Comics; 1989

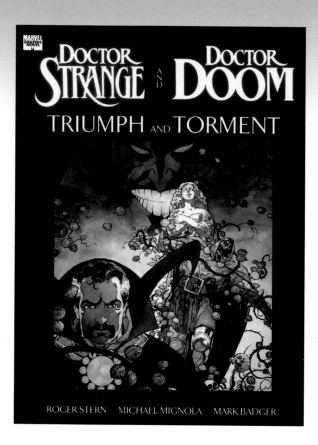

As a storytelling form that's traditionally serialized, most of the greatest superhero graphic novels are actually collections of specific comic book issues. *Triumph and Torment*, however, is the rare example of a superhero story constructed as a graphic novel from the start, a format which lends its author and artists the time and space necessary to tell as epic of a story as they desire.

Triumph and Torment gives a glimpse beneath the armored shell of one of Marvel Comics' most iconic villains, Doctor Victor Von Doom.[10] After a contest of supernatural strength declares Doctor Strange as Earth's Sorcerer Supreme, he's tasked with granting aid to Earth's #2 sorcerer—Doctor Doom—and, surprisingly, rather than turn away the aid, the proud Doom enlists Strange to assist him in doing the one thing he can't do alone—save his mother's soul from the clutches of the underworld.

While Doctor Strange is the obvious hero of this piece, Doctor Doom is definitely its main character. Previous depictions of Doom showcased his ability to be power-hungry, tyrannical, and everything else you could ever want out of a megalomaniacal villain.

Roger Stern stays loyal to Doom's history while deepening our understanding of him, showing glimpses of a man beneath the armor, one willing to endure any pain for the sake of achieving his

---

10 Whose last name is seriously Doom in one of comics most obvious cases of nominative determinism. With a surname like Doom, what else was the guy to do but become a supervillain? Can't become a manager at a Staples with a name like that.

goals. Stern draws parallels between Strange's quest for recovery after the car accident which crippled him and Doom's quest for power; while Strange searched for tranquility and meaning to his life, Doom desired strength above all else in order to retake his homeland of Latveria. Doom's mother felt a similar lust for power; when she and his father were cast from Latveria for the crime of being minorities, she made a deal with Mephisto—Marvel Comics' Faustian, Satanic figure. Once the deal was struck she found the power uncontrollable, and opted for self-sacrifice rather than risking harm to more innocents. Since then Doom has obsessed over rescuing her from Mephisto's clutches, unable to do it alone, but too proud to ever ask for help.

Though it's hardly a subtle piece, *Triumph and Torment* delivers a bombastic adventure from start to finish. Mike Mignola and Mark Badger's art depicts arcane bolts and demonic forces so colorfully they glow off the page; Stern's script captures the essence of Mephisto, the ruler of Hell, and Doctors Strange and Doom as the larger-than-life characters they are.

"Despite its flaws, Doctor Strange and Doctor Doom: Triumph and Torment is emotionally moving, philosophically intriguing, theatrical, and superbly-composed by two artistic innovators coming together like contrapuntal melodies."[11]

—John Parker, Comics Alliance

Ever since his mother made a pact with Mephisto, Doctor Doom is obsessed with rescuing her from the Faustian figure.

---

11 Quote from: http://comicsalliance.com/doctor-strange-doctor-doom-triumph-and-torment-review-marvel/.

GOD LOVES, MAN KILLS

Written by: Chris Claremont • Art by: Brent Anderson • Publisher: Marvel Comics; 1982

Over the years, the X-Men have been many things: teachers, renegades, dimension-hopping adventurers, and harbingers of the Apocalypse,[12] just to name a few. However, at their core, they're a group of minority heroes fighting to protect a world that largely condemns them. Few writers know these characters and their core concept as well as Chris Claremont, and his seminal work, *God Loves, Man Kills*, illustrates this band of mutant heroes at their finest.

Reverend Stryker and his Purifiers are obsessed with "purifying" the Earth of its mutant populace. Like most cult leaders, Stryker twists traditional religion to suit his needs, while smooth-talking non-believers into seeing things his way. His ultimate goal is the extinction of the mutant race, making the X-Men and Charles Xavier, the most public figures on the mutant front, his first targets.

Claremont decompresses action and story in a way that's lightning fast and easy to digest while still giving time for each character's unique voice to shine. Nightcrawler is light-hearted, yet existential, and haunted by his past, Kitty Pryde's youthful and

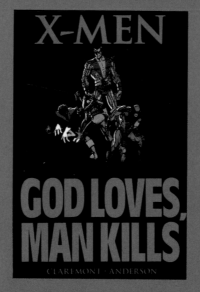

passionate, Wolverine's ... well, he's mostly just gruff.

In the climactic, televised showdown against Reverend Stryker, the X-Men try to foil his plans peacefully. Cyclops delivers an impassioned, idealistic speech that shakes Stryker and strikes the hearts and minds of those listening. While Stryker talks of racism and eugenics, Cyclops speaks of cooperation and moving forward. It's this willingness to touch on so many real social issues which enables *God Loves, Man Kills* to hold up over time. The hateful anti-mutant actions and comments seen throughout *God Loves, Man Kills* continue to parallel the ever-evolving face of bigotry. It's an unfortunate fact that most human conflict derives from xenophobia, the fear of those different than us. The X-Men have always been characters who helped shine a light on that xenophobia, illustrating that bigots aren't always evil—sometimes they're merely misguided or poorly educated. And the people these bigots fear the most, no matter how different they are, even if they have blue fur and can teleport or adamantium claws and a penchant for calling people "bub," are just *people*.

12 And harbingers of the mutant Apocalypse, a dude so bad he named himself after the end of the world.

Magneto gets harsh; the X-Men wax poetic.

FIVE SUPERHERO GRAPHIC NOVELS THAT NEED TO BECOME MOVIES

The rise of the superhero movie brought with it the rise of adapting superhero graphic novels to film. *X2: X-Men United*'s adaptation of *God Loves, Man Kills* is but one example of filmmakers mining a book's history to bring its best stories to life. Superhero fans have been thrilled to see so many of their favorite spandex-clad heroes smashing bad guys and spitting quippy little quips, some still hunger for more. We want to see more unusual superhero stories, ones which take more of our favorite storylines overlooked by the general public and give them the big-budget film treatment, so here are a few excellent superhero books (not mentioned elsewhere in the book) which deserve a shot at the silver screen.

5. DEADPOOL & CABLE

Written by: Fabian Nicieza & Reilly Brown
Art by: Mark Brooks, Patrick Zircher, Lan Medina, Reilly Brown, Ron Lim, Staz Johnson, and Jon Malin

The Merc with the Mouth teams up with the Guy with the Glowing Eye to shoot people and argue—it's a match made in buddy-cop heaven. As a Super-Serious Guy from a Super-Serious future, Cable makes the perfect foil for Deadpool's fourth wall-breaking, pop culture-reference-making antics as they smash their way through mutant hunters, bizarre supervillains, and even the occasional superhero. While most comic book heroes stay (relatively) squeaky clean, these two are more than willing to get their hands dirty doing the morally questionable stuff, which makes for fascinating viewing.

After years of fighting 20th Century Fox to get *Deadpool* made, star Ryan Reynolds brought fans the first real on-screen appearance of the Merc with the Mouth (No, *The Wolverine* doesn't count. He didn't have a mouth for like half that movie). The wacky, hilarious, ultra-violent *Deadpool* went on to become the most financially successful R-rated film of all time, opening to a whopping $152 million at the box office and netting a smooth $746 million for its entire global run.

4. GUARDIANS OF THE GALAXY: LEGACY

Written by: Dan Labnett & Andy Lanning • Art by: Paul Pelletier

The unexpected success of *Guardians of the Galaxy*[13] (which clobbered the 2014 box office by making more than $773 million globally) led to inevitable sequels, cartoons, and merchandising deals. *Guardians* went pretty wild with its *Star Wars*-esque space-action antics, but fans want to see bigger, better, *crazier* antics. *Legacy* has space battles, cosmic god beings, and bald, telekinetic martial artist ladies (okay, just the one bald telekinetic martial artist lady). It's a wild book, but at its core are the *Guardians* characters audiences grew to love, and the strong characterization from Labnet and Lanning help create the oddly human characterization of inhuman characters that the series is known for.

Guardians of the Galaxy: Legacy—more Groot, extra filling!

13 Unexpected by many, anyway. Marvel knew *Guardians* was going to be big because they've got psychics in their employ or something.

3. BATGIRL OF BURNSIDE

Written by: Cameron Stewart & Brenden Fletcher • Art by: Babs Tarr

Fast, fun, and full of heart, *Batgirl of Burnside* takes one of DC Comics' most well-known superheroes and transforms her, putting her in a hip young setting that's primed for lighthearted superhero antics. Cameron Stewart and Brenden Fletcher do a fantastic job of making Barbara Gordon a fascinatingly complicated character, one who's fun to watch kicking butts or thinking #deepthoughts. Babs Tarr's Batgirl redesign, which places practicality over traditional superheroine vacuum-sealed spandex sex appeal, would be easy to translate to film, and with the way her bright, kinetic art practically moves off the page, making a live-action (or animated) feature of it is practically a must.

2. SPIDER-GWEN: MOST WANTED

Written by: Jason Latour • Art by: Robbi Rodriguez

1. MILES MORALES: ULTIMATE SPIDER-MAN COLLECTION

Written by: Brian Michael Bendis & Sara Pichelli
Art by: Sara Pichelli

In each of these stories, we get new versions of one of comicdom's most famous heroes. In *Spider-Gwen*, the girl most known as Spider-Man's dead girlfriend instead becomes Spider-Woman, web-slinging her way around New York City while wrestling with her own eternal bad luck and the guilt she feels over Peter Parker's death.

In *Ultimate Spider-Man*, young Miles Morales acquires Spider-Man-esque abilities, and decides to fight crime while trying to live up to the legacy of the deceased original Spider-Man.[14]

With a half-a-dozen-ish films (and almost as many continuity reboots) in a single decade, many fans have grown tired of seeing Peter Parker repeatedly don the spider-threads. Spider-Gwen and Miles Morales come from incredibly popular comics, bringing new twists to the classic Spider-Man tale while bringing their own quirks and stories. Plus, they represent non-white, non-male individuals in a way that's sadly lacking in most superhero films—not all superheroes need to be played by white guys named Chris, *Marvel*.

14 This is a different dead Peter Parker/Spider-Man than the dead Peter Parker Spider-Gwen is guilt-ridden over. You see, both *Miles Morales: Ultimate Spider-Man* and *Spider-Gwen* take place in alternate universes, separate from each other and the traditional Marvel Comics Universe (known as Earth 616), although, after the events of Marvel's "Secret Wars" Miles Morales actually ends up ... You know what? Forget explaining all this. Stuff like this is why non-superhero comics fans think the genre's hard to get into sometimes.

THE DARK KNIGHT RETURNS

Written by: Frank Miller • Art by: Frank Miller, Klaus Janson, and Lynn Varley • Publisher: DC Comics; 1986

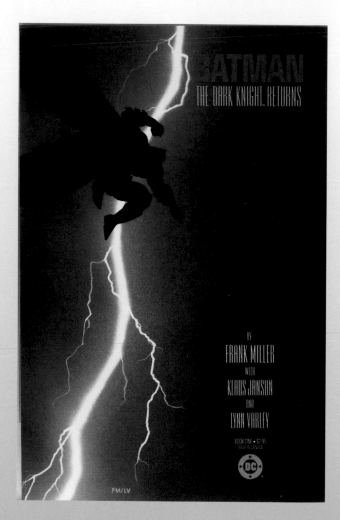

In the grim darkness of Gotham City, chaos reigns. Gangs overrun the city, dangerous super-criminals run free, supposedly "rehabilitated" by those soft enough to believe such falsehoods, and the citizens live in fear. The Batman hung up his cape and cowl years ago, but a (Bat)man can only sit idly by for so long. *The Dark Knight* returns to Gotham in an edgy take on one of pop culture's most iconic heroes.

Frank Miller's Batman is grizzled, gritty, and pessimistic. He relishes in the pain of his foes, and is more concerned with contests of masculinity than acts of heroism. Like much of Miller's work, *maleness* is a pervasive element to *The Dark Knight Returns*. Batman, Superman, the Mutant gang members, even the normally spindly Joker, are all barrel-chested slabs of muscle who solve conflicts with the most brutal of brute force. Gone are the bright colors, silly villains, or selfless ideals of previous iterations. The weighty line work and frequently rigid, grid-oriented panel layouts build a hard, almost oppressive, feel to the story. *The Dark Knight Returns* reflects the zeitgeist of 1980s popular culture—it's dark, seemingly bereft of hope, critical of the increasingly vapid consumer culture popularized by dumbed-down news and entertainment. Miller stated that *The Dark Knight Returns* was directly inspired by other hyperviolent stories of the time, saying, "Now it was the very angry late '70s, early '80s, the time of *Dirty Harry* and *Death Wish*."[15] He later added, "I had to adapt to survive and that involved some changes inside myself, changes which contributed to the macho fantasy of the street vigilante."[16]

Reading *The Dark Knight Returns* now, much like seeing any seminal work long after its premiere, makes for an odd experience. The artistic style, mood, and voice of the comic have been aped so many times, and are played with such utter seriousness, that there are moments it feels almost like a parody of itself.

Whether you agree with Miller's controversial take on Batman or not, his deconstruction was a reverberating presence felt throughout the comics world for years to come, helping create what is often referred to as the "Dark Age of Comics."

This is not the mud wrestling you're looking for.

15 Retrieved from: http://www.nydailynews.com/entertainment/tv-movies/frank-miller-dark-knight-brought-batman-back-life-article-1.351685.
16 *Graphic Novels: Everything You Need to Know* by Paul Gravett.

THE ADVENTURES OF SUPERHERO GIRL

Written by/art by: Faith Erin Hicks • Publisher: Dark Horse Comics; 2013

The Avengers make being a superhero look like a constant thrill ride. You get to live in a cool, multi-million dollar facility, have access to all the high-techiest of gadgets and awesomest superpowers, and go toe-to-toe with the fiercest villains in the universe. But what about the street-level superheroes, the ones doing the little things The Avengers are too busy to do, like stopping supermarket ninjas or rescuing cats from trees? That's where Superhero Girl comes in, putting right what once went (slightly) wrong.

The Adventures of Superhero Girl smartly parodies typical superhero stories with Faith Erin Hicks' effortlessly charming characters and her knowledge of superheroic tropes. Superhero Girl doesn't battle world-ending cosmic forces or terrorist organizations; she faces off against The Marsh Mallow Menace (who is about as threatening as he sounds) and a guy whose power is that he can make people think he's awesome. She rarely remembers to take off her mask when switching to her secret identity, which leaves her with really funky tan lines sometimes. Other people constantly harangue her about her lack of a tragic backstory—her parents are both happy and healthy, and she wasn't crippled by a scientific accident to gain her powers. She just likes being a superhero, and that's that. The constant questioning Superhero Girl gets from those claiming she's not a "real" superhero (questioning her superhero brother, Kevin, never gets) could also be seen as a metaphor for the ongoing "fake geek girl" elitist controversy broiling in parts of the comics world. Because Superhero Girl doesn't fit certain "rules" others have predefined for what makes up

a superhero, they dismiss her, in much the same way that some comics nerds try to dismiss people, especially nerdy girls, from being part of what was traditionally thought of as a straight white boy's club.

Overall, Superhero Girl's world isn't about making hard choices, or battling inner darkness. It's about being a good person when you get the chance, or making nice conversation with surprisingly polite, chatty villains (they're Canadian, which explains it).

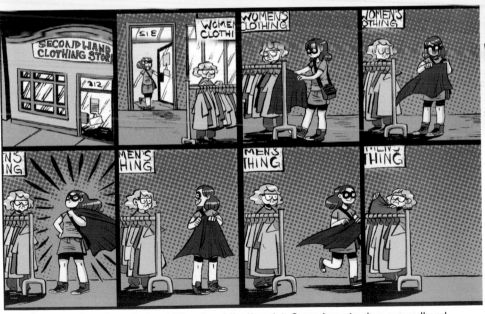

Not every superhero is a playboy billionaire philanthropist. Some have to shop secondhand.

KINGDOM COME

Written by: Mark Waid • Story by/art by: Alex Ross • Publisher: DC Comics; 1996

If *The Dark Knight Returns* and *Watchmen* deconstructed the superhero genre, *Kingdom Come*, it could be argued, reconstructed it. Set some time in the ambiguous future, *Kingdom Come* features DC's classic superheroes in their later years. Here they've ascended beyond things like "secret identities" to become the most powerful versions of themselves. Superman's strength and invulnerability seem to have no limit. The Flash has become one with the speed force and transformed into a being of pure speed, righting wrongs fractions of an instant after they start happening. Batman ... well, he's a grumpy old man in his cave, but he's also got an army of Bat-mechs kicking ass all around Gotham city. The power of these heroes' legacy extends beyond their mortal grasp; they're not just people with powers fighting for what's right, they're *symbols*.

Most of *Kingdom Come* centers around the conflicts between the old guard superheroes, who won't compromise their morals and change with the times, and the new generation of younger, brasher heroes—the sort of superheroes overpopulating the pages of '90s comics. These younger, totally extreme heroes fly off the handle, ready to fight anyone and anything regardless of how many innocent bystanders are hurt. *They* argue that their methods are necessary to battle the increasingly extreme supervillains of their time. Superman and his amazing friends beg to differ.

At the surface, this is a clash of old-school versus

new-school mentalities, but beneath it is an examination of the superhero as an icon. In their refusal to yield to the increasing moral ambiguities of modern conflicts, Superman and his ilk illustrate why they've managed to be such compelling characters for so long. The Man of Steel is nearly a century old, and yet, week after week, writers keep writing new stories about him because the core of this hero is so universal—he's a symbol for hope, for goodness no matter the personal cost, and an inspiration to others. *Kingdom Come*'s numerous other characters all contribute toward a common theme of maintaining hope while moving forward (without forgetting the past). The deific art of Alex Ross captures a realism to these larger-than-life characters even when they're hurling lightning or moving faster than a speeding bullet.

Throughout *Kingdom Come* we see all sorts of legacy heroes—sons and daughters with powers and skills of their own, inspired by the generation before them to do what's right even when it's not easy—mirroring the way we continue to see audiences and creators alike become inspired by these characters who ascend beyond mere bits of ink to become something bigger. Something symbolic. Something *super*.

BEHIND THE INK: ALEX ROSS

In a time of steroid-infused male physiques and women whose bodies looked like hips and breasts attached to broken spines, Alex Ross instead opted to create images of breathtaking, superheroic realism, putting him head and shoulders above the zeitgeist of '90s

PROMINENT WORKS:
• *Marvels* (1994)
• *Kingdom Come* (1996)
• *JLA Secret Origins* (2002)

mainstream comics. Ross makes heavy use of photo references, painting images of super-beings who look like they could be real people in a style that's been described as "Norman Rockwell meets George Perez."[17]

He's a famously meticulous artist, generally creating iconic cover images rather than page-by-page content due to the enormous time it takes to paint each of his astonishing works. Ross is a longtime student of comics, and cites John Romita Jr., Neal Adams, and Jack Kirby as heavily influential to him. Ross describes Kirby in particular as being "The Picasso of comics. He took the form from an infancy stage—you know, the basic illustrations—to all different levels till eventually creating his own form of art out of the language of comics. Also, his expression was indigenous to comics; the energy that he gave comics was unlike anything else, anywhere else."[18]

17 http://www.avclub.com/article/reinventing-the-pencil-21-artists-who-changed-main-30528.
18 *The Jack Kirby Collector*, Kirby & Morrow.

Alex Ross Avengers/Invaders #2 cover painting original art (Marvel, 2008). In this tale of time-tossed heroes, The Golden Age Invaders (Namor the Sub-Mariner, Captain America, Bucky, Toro, and the Human Torch) show up in the modern day Marvel-U ... and are soundly thrashed by the then-current Avengers line-up of the Sentry, Ares (God of War), Iron Man, Wonder Man, and Ms. Marvel. Ross' original art sold for $10,157 at Heritage Auctions.

EX MACHINA

Written by: Brian K. Vaughan • Art by: Tony Harris • Publisher: Vertigo; 2014

Being in charge isn't easy. Being in charge of New York City, the greatest city of Earth (depending on who you ask) right after 9/11 when you're an ex-superhero whose old days and old ways are always trying to push themselves back into your new life, well, that's a job no one would want. No one except Mitchell Hundred, that is.

The attacks of September 11th changed America forever, often in ways few could have predicted. *Ex Machina* depicts some of the earliest thoughts on these changes with its depiction of a post-terrorism New York City struggling to maintain its sense of normalcy in a newly-uprooted world.

Despite the fact that Hundred is, at his core, a superhero, superpowers are not the focus here, as this is a tale about the power to incite change—superheroic, political, or otherwise—covering a bevy of topics like terrorism, gay marriage, racial inequality, educational overhaul, and whether it's okay to paint racist words over a picture of Abe Lincoln and call it art. Brian K. Vaughan's wandering narrative structure gives the story the freedom to tackle tough topics, using superheroics to put them under the microscope without getting particularly preachy about it.

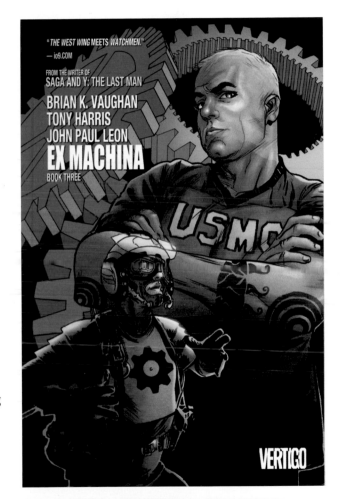

"*THE WEST WING MEETS WATCHMEN.*"
— io9.COM

FROM THE WRITER OF
SAGA AND Y: THE LAST MAN
BRIAN K. VAUGHAN
TONY HARRIS
JOHN PAUL LEON
EX MACHINA
BOOK THREE

VERTIGO

"YOU ARE THE CHIEF EXECUTIVE OF NEW YORK CITY, NOT MOTHERF***ING ROBOCOP."
—POLICE COMMISSIONER ANGOTTI

V FOR VENDETTA

Written by: Alan Moore • Art by: David Lloyd • Publisher: Vertigo; 2008

"Remember, remember the fifth of November!" Why? Because it's Gunpowder Treason Day, otherwise known as Guy Fawkes Day.

But what does that really mean? England originally started celebrating this day in 1605 to commemorate the fact that Guy Fawkes and his cohorts failed to blow up the House of Lords when trying to assassinate King James I. Fawkes was discovered guarding thirty six barrels of gun powder underneath the House of Lords, and since there's not really a good way to lie your way out of that one, he was arrested instantly. Guy Fawkes Day began as an anti-Catholic celebration over the Protestant King not being blown to pieces. Hundreds of years later, some accredit Alan Moore and David Lloyd's *V for Vendetta* for transforming Guy Fawkes' reputation, making him into a symbol of revolutionary heroism rather than the traitor he was often referred to as.

V for Vendetta is set in an alternate London in 1998, one where a fascist government has taken over. Moore introduces the mysterious V, a man clad all in black save for a Guy Fawkes mask, by having him save a young woman from corrupt government officials, then blowing up the Houses of Parliament—completing Guy Fawkes' centuries-old plan. What unfolds from there is the story of one man trying to inspire civilians to rise up against injustices being enforced by the government.

The creation of V came in a letter from David Lloyd to Alan Moore stating, "I was thinking, why

V: Heroic rebel or terrorist lunatic?

don't we portray him as a resurrected Guy Fawkes...? He'd look really bizarre and it would give Guy Fawkes the image he's deserved all these years. We shouldn't burn the chap every Nov. 5th but celebrate his attempt to blow up Parliament!"[19]

Moore, however, took an ambiguous approach in writing V, poising him as a controversial protagonist who can either be interpreted as a heroic freedom fighter or selfish, insane traitor. Moore applied this level of thoughtfulness throughout *V for Vendetta*, crafting a provoking and poetic work filled with allegorical references to literature and music, all tightly put together to provide sharp, deliberate commentary on the seemingly-endless corruption of politics.

19 Moore, Alan (1988). *Behind The Painted Smile*.

The 1980s were a bleak time in most parts of the globe. The Cold War loomed over us, Ronald Reagan's terrible economic policies were crushing the middle and lower classes, and someone had the genius idea to greenlight *Cop Rock*, the musical police procedural. That bleakness infiltrated the pop culture landscape. Even comic books, which had traditionally been upbeat sources of lighthearted adventure, took a turn for the dark, and *Watchmen* was both a reaction to, and a part of, that turn. *Watchmen* took apart the superhero genre, exposing its grimy, gritty parts through the dirty lens of reality. Superheroes, as it turned it, could exist without being super or heroes.

Never short on words or storylines, Alan Moore weaves together the tales of a number of different superheroes as they investigate a conspiracy that leaves one of them dead. Rorschach leads the investigation with his trademark mask, coat, and ruthless adherence to self-imposed rules. He is, to put it in *Dungeons and Dragons* terms, a perfect example of Lawful Neutral; good and evil are concepts that don't matter to him. The only thing he cares about is sticking to his own moral code (which happens to put him on the side of the good guys, sort of). He's a creep and a lunatic; despite a few surface similarities to Batman, he acts in decidedly

WATCHMEN

ALAN MOORE
DAVE GIBBONS

All the whores and politicians will look up and shout, 'Save us!' and I'll down and whisper ... 'No.'"

the while raring for a fight and ignoring the fact that they didn't seem to know anything.

As the only member of the Watchmen with actual superpowers, Dr. Manhattan serves as a Superman analogue, only his abilities have ascended him to the point of detaching him from humanity. Nite Owl's arguably the most heroic member of the group, but he's still kind of a wimp, and way too much of

a fanboy over the superheroes of generations past. Rorschach, Dr. Manhattan, Nite Owl, and the rest of the caped crusaders of Watchmen all provide different viewpoints with which to take apart the traditional idea of a superhero; their selfish motivations and immoral methods make them far removed from the idealistic icons you'll find in most comics.

While *Watchmen*'s bold, gritty take on a well-tread

genre was a much-needed, reflective story, its success (along with the success of Frank Miller's *The Dark Knight Returns*) lead to much of the comics industry trying to copycat that grittiness without any thought to it, leading to the pervasive terribleness of '90s mainstream comics. Every hero was more extreme, more vicious, no black was black enough for the blackness of their souls and the blackness of their violence. Conversely, *Watchmen* also encouraged both fans and writers alike to think of superheroes from more critical angles, analyzing them more deeply and, in turn, creating stronger stories that better reflect the human condition.

"Watchmen's *influence on comics and comic book culture can't be overstated—its self-aware, adult sensibility has become so pervasive that it's difficult to list titles that haven't adopted it.*"[20]
—The Paley Center for Media

"*The most profound and influential challenge to the idealized, nationalist logic of superhero comics was Alan Moore's* Watchmen, *in which he treats the desire for surveillance and salvation manifested by costumed saviors as tools of a fascist state.*"[21]
— Dr. Rebecca Wanzo

Rorschach harasses a retired supervillain for information.

20 Quote retrieved from: http://www.paleycenter.org/watchmen-watchmens-legacy/.
21 *The Superhero: Meditations on Surveillance, Salvation, and Desire. Journal:*

THE KILLING JOKE

Written by: Alan Moore • Art by: Brian Bolland • Publisher: DC Comics; 1988

Commissioner Gordon's had a pretty bad day. His daughter's been shot and paralyzed, he's been kidnapped, and to top it all off, he's stuck listening to this lunatic clown ramble on about the nature of sanity and order. It's almost enough to drive a man mad ...

And that's exactly what The Joker is counting on.

Alan Moore's and Brian Bolland's groundbreaking graphic novel presents the modern-day Joker's attempt to break Gordon's mind by pushing him to the very limit while diving into the Clown Prince of Crime's (supposed) history to show the one bad day, which transformed him into what he is. At the other end of the spectrum stands Batman, the order to Joker's chaos, who'll be damned if he lets that clown do any more harm.

Based on Joseph Campbell's archetypal monomyth story structure, the main villain of any story is going to be a Shadow of the Hero—a dark reflection of who that hero is. Here we see one of the strongest depictions of The Joker as Batman's Shadow; while Batman stands for order, helping others to not live through the same kind of tragedy that made him into what he is, the Joker relishes chaos and craves the idea of living in a world where everyone is as mad as he.

Batgirls in Boxes, Women in Refrigerators

The Killing Joke also broke new ground due to its treatment of Barbara Gordon—otherwise known as Batgirl—by putting her in the oft-maligned category of being a "woman in a refrigerator." The phrase, "women in refrigerators," refers to the

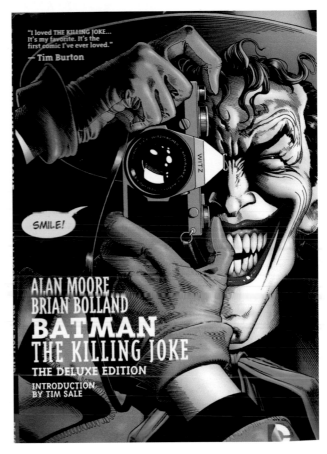

alarming frequency with which female characters are killed/maimed/depowered to serve as part of a male character's story rather than as part of the female character's own story. Comic book writer Gail Simone derived the phrase from an incident wherein Green Lantern Kyle Raynor's girlfriend, Alexandra Dewitt, was murdered and stuffed into a refrigerator

The Joker tries his gloved hand at real estate.

by a supervillain. Barbara Gordon's paralysis, inflicted on her by The Joker as a means of breaking Commissioner Gordon's mind, is another high-profile example of this disturbingly common trend. Though fictional male characters go through plenty of their own suffering, they generally do it as part of their own stories and get to bounce back from whatever form of death/depowering they've suffered. Female characters often do not. "If you demolish most of the characters girls like," argues Simone, "the girls won't read comics."[22]

On the plus side, this "fridging" of Barbara Gordon had some positive impact. After the incident, now bound to a wheelchair, Barbara became The Oracle, an information-gathering hero and one of the few depictions of handicapped superheroes in comic books.

22 Quote retrieved from: https://en.wikipedia.org/wiki/Women_in_Refrigerators.

Some days, you just can't get rid of a clown.

BEHIND THE INK: ALAN MOORE

We'll dim the lights on this spotlight so we don't scare off the reclusive, cantankerous writer Alan Moore. Moore's long career has produced many of the greatest works in graphic novel history; pages upon pages of our book is devoted to his creations. He's a famously odd man, with his scruffy, unkempt appearance and penchant for anarchy, but he's also an astonishing judge of human behavior, able to keenly craft stories which are as vivid as they are wise. He's famously had a number of his works adapted into films, and publicly denounced each of them, having his name removed from them as to disassociate himself from these tainted portrayals of his work.

Film Adaptations of Alan Moore Novels the Grumpy Old Codger Had His Name Removed From

From Hell (2001)

Why? Because the filmmakers wanted to make a bunch of radical changes, like making the main character into young and sexy Johnny Depp instead of a craggy old dude.

The League of Extraordinary Gentlemen (2003)

Why? Because, again, the filmmakers wanted to make a bunch of changes he didn't like. To be fair, having seen *The League of Extraordinary Gentlemen*, he probably made the right call—that flick's a freaking mess.

V for Vendetta (2005)

Why? Because, Moore said, the Wachowski's interpretation of his graphic novel missed the point of the original entirely by excluding "things like fascism and anarchy. Those words, 'fascism' and 'anarchy,' occur nowhere in the film. It's been turned into a Bush-era parable by people too timid to set a political satire in their own country."[23]

Constantine (2005)

Why? Because, at that point, he'd been so miffed at previous adaptations of his work that he asked any future adaptations have his name excised from them.

Watchmen (2009)

Why? Because "there are things that we did with *Watchmen* that could only work in a comic, and were indeed designed to show off things that other media can't."[24] Like the rest of the adaptations of his work, he never saw *Watchmen*, though he did state that the original script penned by David Hayter of *Metal Gear Solid* fame was "as close as I could imagine anyone getting to *Watchmen*."[25]

Probably Anything Else He Ever Does (From now until the end of eternity)

Why? Because he's a grumpy old codger, that's why.

23 Retrieved from: http://www.mtv.com/shared/movies/interviews/m/moore_alan_060315/.
24 Gopalan, Nisha (July 16, 2008). "Alan Moore Still Knows the Score!" *Entertainment Weekly*.
25 Jensen, Jeff (October 25, 2005). "Watchmen: An Oral History." *Entertainment Weekly*.

Movie producers often look at film adaptations as easy money. "There's a built-in fanbase," they chortle through a cloud of cigar smoke and aspiring actor tears, "and we already got a story to work with. Half the work's already done!" The truth, however, is that sometimes stories which work in one format don't work in another. Or sometimes the filmmakers adapting these properties have no idea what they're doing, and make a bunch of idiotic changes. Or sometimes the original properties kind of sucked to begin with, and there wasn't much to be done. For whatever reason, for every great graphic novel-turned-film, there are plenty which aren't so great, so we've gathered up five of the stinkiest pieces of cinematic cheese for your scornful pleasure.

5.

Graphic Novel: Whiteout
Written by: Greg Rucka • Art by: Steve Lieber
Film adaptation: Whiteout (2009)

WHY IT'S THE WORST: This mystery lacks mystery, it's slower than the arctic glaciers of its Antarctic setting, and more rigidly formulaic than a group of uptight mathematicians, who haven't gotten laid in 3.14 decades. Plus the film studio producing it, in all its infinite wisdom, decided that having two female leads was one woman too many, and altered the cast to a single lady.

4.

Graphic Novel: A Dame to Kill For
Written by/art by: Frank Miller
Film adaptation: Sin City: A Dame to Kill For (2014)

WHY IT'S THE WORST: It's so stylish and so weird, bearing a comic book color scheme, dominatrix gunslingers, and at times cartoonish violence, and yet *Sin City: A Dame to Kill For* commits the most heinous offense a film can: it's *boring*. Audiences and critics alike yawned their way through every screening; *A Dame to Kill For* felt like a soulless retread of Rodriguez/Miller's *Sin City*, only with worse plotting, pacing, and even more lunkheaded characterization throughout.

KATE BECKINSALE

WHITEOUT
SEE YOUR LAST BREATH.

WARNER BROS. PICTURES PRESENTS
IN ASSOCIATION WITH DARK CASTLE ENTERTAINMENT A DOMINIC SENA FILM KATE BECKINSALE "WHITEOUT" GABRIEL MACHT COLUMBUS SHORT AND TOM SKERRITT
MUSIC BY JOHN FRIZZELL COSTUME DESIGNER GRAHAM "GRACE" WALKER EDITOR MARTIN HUNTER DIRECTOR OF PHOTOGRAPHY CHRIS SOOS A.C.S. EXECUTIVE PRODUCERS RICHARD MIRISCH ADAM KUHN
ASSOCIATE PRODUCER STEVE RICHARDS DON CARMODY GREG RUCKA BASED ON THE GRAPHIC NOVEL WRITTEN BY GREG RUCKA AND STEVE LIEBER PUBLISHED BY ONI PRESS
SCREENPLAY BY JON HOEBER & ERICH HOEBER AND CHAD HAYES & CAREY W. HAYES DIRECTED BY DOMINIC SENA
SEPTEMBER

3. Graphic Novel: The Crow

Written by/art by: James O'Barr
Film adaptation: The Crow: Wicked Prayer (2005)

WHY IT'S THE WORST: This one is a bit of a stretch seeing as how it's a sequel to a film adapted from *The Crow*, but it sucks so unbelievably hard it merits mentioning anyway. This straight-to-video impacted fecal matter stars David "Don't Call Me Angel" Boreanaz, Edward "Don't Call Me John Connor" Furlong, Dennis "Don't Call Me Koopa" Hopper, and Tara "Just Call Me Whatever, Don't Call Me Sharknado" Reid. This terrible retread of the dour *Crow* story is the lowest point in the careers of most involved, made a fraction of what it cost, and, to quote Wikipedia, was "critically panned, currently holding a 0% approval at Rotten Tomatoes.com."[26]

2. Graphic Novel: 300's sequel Xerxes

A work by Frank Miller which is, as of this writing, incomplete
Film adaptation: 300: Rise of an Empire (2009)

WHY IT'S THE WORST: This dumb sequel to a not-particularly-cerebral film was such a hackneyed retread that its director, Noam Murro, a.k.a the poor man's Zack Snyder, had to change the color of everyone's capes from the red of the original to blue in order to remind audiences that, yes, this is technically a different movie. Very few members of the original cast returned (an unusually smart choice for the hit-and-miss Gerard Butler), leaving audiences perpetually bored by the second-string actors trying desperately to live up to the over-the-top performances of the original. Film critic Todd Gilchrist described the film by saying, "*Rise of an Empire* lacks director Snyder's shrewd deconstruction of cartoonish hagiography, undermining the glorious, robust escapism of testosterone-fueled historical reenactment with an underdog story that's almost too reflective to be rousing."[27]

1. Graphic Novel: The League of Extraordinary Gentlemen

Written by: Alan Moore • **Art by:** Kevin O'Neill
Film adaptation: The League of Extraordinary Gentlemen (2003)

WHY IT'S THE WORST: Okay, honestly, *The League of Extraordinary Gentlemen* takes a beating from damn near everyone. Alan Moore hates it because it bears almost no resemblance to his original story, critics hated it because it's a twisting, turning mess with too many characters, subplots, pointless action, and ill thought out writing, and audiences hated it because it's essentially a C-list movie starring mostly B-list actors trying to make an A-list summer blockbuster. And they're all right— *The League of Extraordinary Gentlemen* is one dumbass film. Still, there's an odd charm to its stupidity, and it's got a high energy throughout most of its running time, pushing it for many from simply being a "bad" film into becoming a "so bad it's ironically kind of good" film.

26 Quote retrieved from: https://en.wikipedia.org/wiki/The_Crow:_Wicked_Prayer.

27 Quote retrieved from: http://www.thewrap.com/300-rise-empire-review/.

CHAPTER 2

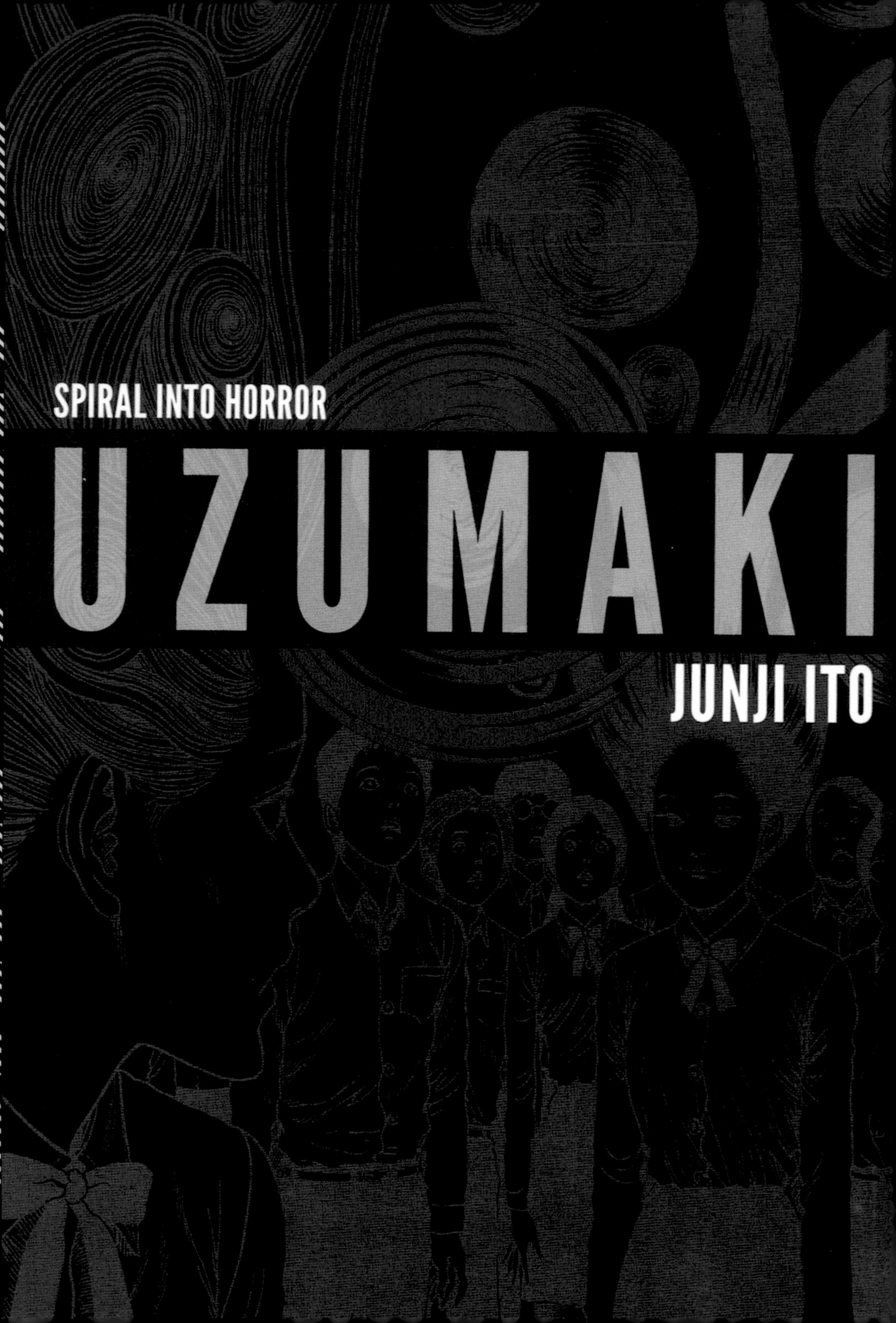

SPIRAL INTO HORROR
UZUMAKI
JUNJI ITO

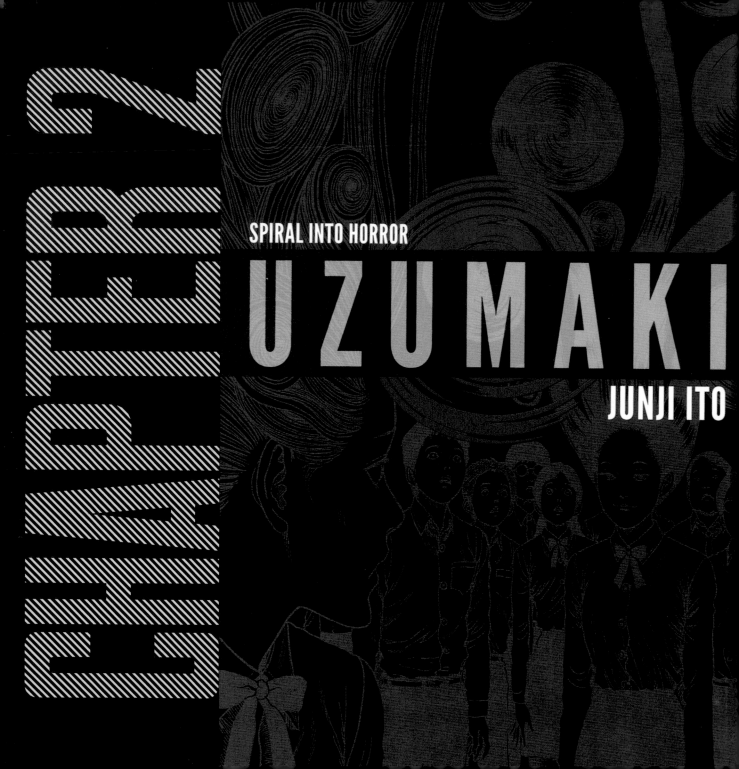

HORROR: THE MACABRE REFLECTION

//////////////////////////

We fear that which we don't understand. Actually, we fear a lot of things. Spiders. The dark. Heights. Speaking in public. Masked lunatics with chainsaws. Being afraid is a heady, potent experience, and genuine fear is pretty unpleasant. Yet, fear also sends a rush of endorphins into our systems, making us feel fast, strong, and *alive*. Horror fiction lets readers experience the thrills of genuine fear without the actual risk involved, giving us a sample of that adrenaline rush without the nastiness of worrying whether that spider is poisonous, whether a fall from this height will kill us instantly, or how well that chainsaw-wielding lunatic can see through his mask. With fiction we get to be pleasantly spooked, then put the book back on the shelf (or in the freezer) when everything's over. Fiction helps us to better understand those things which scare us so that, when the time comes for us to face them in the real world, maybe we won't be so scared anymore.

Comics have a long and lustrous history of inspiring the heebie-jeebies in readers, starting

with Prize Comics' *New Adventures of Frankenstein,* an ongoing series about the monster from Mary Shelley's seminal horror novel, *Frankenstein,* and *Classic Comics* #13[28], which featured an adaptation of *Strange Case of Dr. Jekyll and Mr. Hyde* in the first purely horror-oriented comic. On the cover, Mr. Hyde towers huge over the fleeing, terrified masses, his scaly green skin and sadistic expression a stark contrast to the crimson dusk and shadowy piles of bodies behind him. Comics readers found this cover and the contents within fascinating; never had they seen a comic so boldly determined to scare them.

Over the next few decades, horror comics flourished. Newsstands filled up with weekly and monthly magazines such as *Eerie, Tales from the Crypt, Tomb of Dracula, Adventure into the Unknown,* and even *Captain America's Weird Tales,* a short-lived rebranding of Marvel Comics' star-spangled hero designed to entice fans of this

28 Gilberton Publications' *Classic Comics #13* (Aug. 1943).

burgeoning genre. Horror comics, like most media at the time, were fairly tame compared to the varied fiction available today. However, there was an ease of accessibility to horror comics that prose lacked, and the stunning art trumped the primitive special effects of the time, so fans looking for a good scare flocked to the medium like zombies to a high school camping trip.

Horror comics continued booming for many years until the arrival of Fred Wertham's *Seduction of the Innocent,* a sensationalist book filled with forged data and accounts which described comic books as tools for seducing children into lives of crime and homosexuality.[29]

Frederick Wertham Tried to Kill All Comics

Though Wertham has been largely disregarded for decades, it wasn't until in-depth research by professor Carol Tilley of the University of Illinois that the depths of his falsification were discovered.

"From a contemporary standpoint, *Seduction* is horribly written because it's not documented," said Tilley. "There are no citations, no bibliography. He quotes a lot of people, refers to lots of things, but there's no really good way of knowing what his basis is for any of this."

Tilley's research found mountains of inconsistencies and exaggerations in Wertham's research. *Seduction of the Innocent* is full of secondhand stories Wertham heard from colleagues, facts and data misrepresenting his woefully small sample sizes, and omitted pieces of information

from what few interviews he personally conducted. Wertham, who had spent his life as a clinician working with underprivileged children, genuinely believed that comic books were destroying them, and while what he did was awful and untruthful, his intentions seemed to be good. Still doesn't change the fact that the jerk set the comics industry back decades, though.[30]

After Wertham's fallacious book took America by storm, horror comics, like most of the comics industry, received a massive hit in popularity which took many years to recover from.

In Japan, horror comics suffered no such setback; creators such as Kazuo Umezu were free to create images of terror as they saw fit, leading to seminal works such as *Orochi Blood*, a tale of ghostly hauntings and sororal strife, and *The Drifting Classroom,* an ongoing horror series about a group of fifth- and sixth-graders trying to survive after being transported to a hellish future. Hideshi Hino's *Panorama of Hell* gives an uncomfortable look into a family cursed across generations, employing a morally questionable narrator who speaks directly to the reader to disquieting effect. Go Nagai (*Devilman*) and Hitoshi Iwaaki (*Parasyte*) infused superhero stories with horror, and Junji Ito (*Uzumaki, Tomie, Museum of Terror*) created countless tales of monsters and madness, often ending his stories with his protagonists' fates left ambiguous—a trope common in many Japanese horror stories.

Europe, though not quite as prolific as the United

---

29 Wertham, *Seduction of the Innocent* (1954).

30 Retrieved from: https://news.illinois.edu/blog/view/6367/204890 and http://io9. gizmodo.com/5985199/how-one-mans-lies-almost-destroyed-the-comics-industry.

States or Japan in creating horror comics, did have a few stand-out titles emerge during this slump in American comics. From Italy came Tiziano Sclavi's *Dylan Dog,* an ongoing series about a detective dealing with the supernatural, and numerous sexually-charged horror titles like Barbieri & Bosttoli's *Sukia,* which blended the erotic and the macabre. British Horror comics tended to skew younger, with more light-hearted, humor-oriented stories like *Shiver and Shake* and *Monster Fun,* gently spooky stories reminiscent of Hannah-Barbera cartoons.

Thankfully, the United States eventually began lessening its rules and regulations for comic books, and our favorite tales of vampires, zombies, and were-things began to shuffle their way back into the public consciousness in the 1970s and 1980s. During this time we began to see more complex tales of terror, ones which allowed for sympathetic depictions of typically evil creatures, graphic depictions of death and violence, and tragic stories bereft of comforting happy endings. Heroes born of darkness such as Blade, Swamp Thing, Hellboy, and The Family Circus all thrived. Niche publications like FantaCo Enterprises and Millennium Publications created publishing lineups entirely oriented around horror. Creators were free to create *freely* again, and the genre was richer for it.

In the modern age, those looking for horror comics and graphic novels are privy to the finest selection the world has to offer; thanks to the advent of the internet, it's easier than ever to get your fill of fear from anywhere.

The Ingredients of Fear

Horror writers have broken down the elements of fear into three basic elements: horror[31], disgust, and terror. *Horror* is our fear of bodily harm. We like our bodies, and the idea of some nutcase with a sharp implement hacking it to bits for funsies fills us with dread— something horror writers use to their advantage. *Disgust* is, as you might expect, fear of the vile and putrid. Gory, rotten things which fill our stomachs with unease and compel us to look away, like the decrepit flesh of a zombie or the foul stench of Guy Fieri's food. The most thematically compelling element of horror is *Terror,* the fear of the unknown. That creepy feeling you get on the back of your neck when you're walking alone in the dark, or the itch that makes you wonder if someone is watching you—that's terror. Good horror fiction can use these elements in varying amounts to create different effects. *Severed,* Scott Snyder's cannibal graphic novel, primarily relies on horror and disgust. *Friday the 13th's* masked, machete-wielding Jason Voorhees is mostly horror, with elements of terror to him. The internet-created Slenderman is pure terror; he's a faceless, unknowable being bearing no clear motivation for his child kidnappings. With horror prose, authors have to rely on the reader's imagination to inspire fear; if you become too afraid, you can try to force your imagination to stop. With horror graphic novels, however, the horror is right there on the page, inescapably depicted, with images ready to sear themselves into your brain whether you're ready for them or not. And it's so much fun!

31 Yes, horror writers labeled one of the sub-elements of the horror genre "horror." No, we don't know why they did it, either.

There's an all-consuming loneliness to being a teenager—it's a black hole that sucks away at you, pulling you toward things you don't want to do, twisting you into something you don't want to become. *Black Hole* explores the existential angst of our teenage years through a drug-laced tale of a supernatural sexually-transmitted disease ripping through small-town America during the 1970s.

The unnamed-STD of *Black Hole* spreads simply and quietly, manifesting itself in numerous ways. Rob grows a second mouth (on his neck, just below the shirt line), and Chris' skin sloughs off in huge chunks—and they're the lucky ones. Like the other teens infected with this STD, Rob and Chris suffer shame, paranoia, and isolation. Chris gets the worst of it, moving out into the woods to join other teens whose infections manifested in more obvious ways. She camps endlessly, wasting her days away with thoughts of regret and longing. Human beings are naturally social creatures—we crave social contact the same way we crave food or shelter—and as teenagers, that craving can often overwhelm thoughts of logic or self-preservation.

Charles Burns uses sharp, clear line work and a distinct black-*or*-white style to magnify feelings of unrest and unreality. Often he juxtaposes the detached thoughts of a viewpoint character with the contrasting actions unfolding before them, giving many sequences a dreamy, drugged feeling,

"MAYBE I'M JUST MAKING A BIG DEAL OUT OF IT ... IT'S PROBABLY NOTHING. I'LL BE OK ... I'LL JUST GET MY ACT TOGETHER AND ... I'LL BE OK."
—CHRIS, WHO IS MOST DEFINITELY NOT OKAY.

as if you're being pulled along through a chain of events you neither want any part of nor have any control over. Most of *Black Hole*'s teens are a (deliberately) ugly lot; both they, and most of the world they're in, grow uglier over the course of the story as their conditions worsen. Drug trips and dream sequences grow increasingly intense, with "real" life seeming more disturbing thanks to masterfully bizarre lighting choices. Burns continues to render the world in greater, more disgusting detail as the infected teens slip farther and farther from any semblance of normalcy. *Black Hole*'s blend of horror and teenage angst will likely strike a chord with anyone who remembers what it was like to be a desperate, detached teenager longing for someone who understands and accepts you.

Your guess is as good as ours.

BRAIN CAMP

Written by: Susan Kim & Laurence Klavan • Art by: Faith Erin Hicks • Published by: First Second; 2010

As a kid, even the most controlling parents stay off your back ... for awhile. Once puberty looms close, some parents start to sink their hooks into you to make you their little puppet. "Study now," they say. "Join this club," they'll demand. In small amounts, it can be helpful; at twelve, most of us don't have the foresight to start preparing for your future. In larger doses, however, it can lead to disastrous consequences. You know, typical stuff like panic attacks, kids throwing up from the stress, their heads bulging and ready to explode. Hmm ... okay, maybe that last one's a *little* atypical.

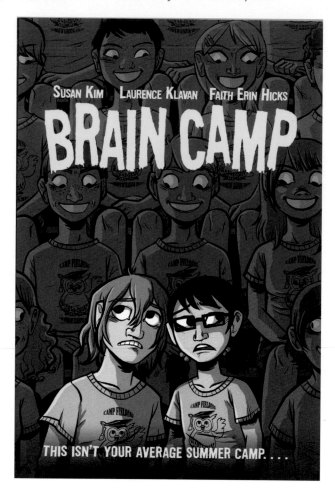

Lucas' alcoholic single mom doesn't pay enough attention to him; Jenna's parents pay a little *too* much attention to her. When the representative from Camp Fielding (aka the Brain Camp) comes knocking, they're all too eager to send their offspring packing to get them out from underfoot and onto the (supposedly) brighter, better path. Things at Brain Camp aren't as nice as they sound, however, with disappearing campers, bizarre food, and a strange teaching curriculum leading these two loners to believe they've been tossed into the bad part of creepytown, and everywhere they turn there's someone trying to entice them to live there with them, *be* like them. Conformity's a major theme of *Brain Camp*, whether it's conforming to the social standards of peers or conforming to the wishes of adults regardless of our own desires. During our pre-teen/teenage years we're often most sensitive to issues of conformity, going along with social norms we ordinarily wouldn't in the desperate hope of fitting in. As adults, many of us face similar issues of conformity, but in a less obvious, more insidious way, with much of society quietly pressuring us into living the way *they* do, following the culturally appropriate path in life (high school, college, job, marriage, house, kids, grandkids, retire, death) and beating the individuality out of us. The way *Brain Camp*'s antagonists constantly focus on traditional, academically-oriented success and the future gives a multifaceted look at conformity at any age.

Brain Camp reads like a more mature, longform version of kids horror shows like *Are You Afraid of the Dark?* (which makes sense, since author Susan Kim wrote for the show). Faith Erin Hicks' clean line work creates a fast-moving story that's easy to read while still managing to contain detailed nuances to warrant a more savory pace.

Brain Camp is the perfect spine-tingler for anyone on the cusp of puberty, on the cusp of being on the cusp of puberty, or who is well past puberty and glad not to have to deal with that crap anymore.

"To be yourself in a world that is constantly trying to change you is the greatest accomplishment."
—Ralph Waldo Emerson

Lucas and Jenna plan an escape.

30 DAYS OF NIGHT

Written by: Steve Niles • Art by: Ben Templesmith • Published by: IDW Publishing; 2007

In a world where vampires exist, the one thing keeping humans safe is the fact that, for all the vamps' eternal life and super-blood-fueled strength, a simple ray of sunlight is enough to turn them to ash. Humans can still get on with their lives during the day, safe and worry-free, and bunker down at night to protect themselves from any unseemly bloodsuckers. But what happens when the sun doesn't shine? Alaska's funky location leaves it in the odd position of experiencing weeks of sunny nights, leading to a lot of lost sleep for the Alaskan people, and weeks of sunless days. When there are vampires around these dark days are every human's worst nightmare ... and every vampire's dream come true.

30 Days of Night tells the story of vampires attacking Alaska during their thirty days of night. Husband and wife, Eben and Stella, call the peaceful little town of Barrow, Alaska, home. That is until some mean, no-good vampires arrive to destroy it all. This concept for a horror story is ingenious in its simplicity—of *course* vampires would attack Alaska during its month-long night. Even if the story were awful (which it isn't), Steve Niles would still deserve recognition for the fact that he came up with such an easy, novel approach to such a well-worn monster.

Like The Flash hopped up on Starbucks, Niles flies through this story at lightning speed, quickly

"NOW YOU'RE CATCHING ON. CHECK ON GUS! BOARD THE WINDOWS! SANDBAG THE DOORS! YOU'LL TRY IT ALL! BUT ONE BY ONE THEY'LL PICK YOU OFF AND STRIP THE MEAT FROM YOUR BONES!"
—A VAMPIRE UP TO NO GOOD

introducing the audience to the main characters, sending them off to investigate some strange happenings, then BAM! Vampires, blood, and death.

Accompanying this unique story is a one-of-a-kind art style by Ben Templesmith. Templesmith opted to forgo the typically good-looking, well-dressed, two-fanged vampire depicted in most popular culture. Instead, Templesmith's vampires are gruesome, horrific creatures, with long, serpentine tongues and rows of shark-like teeth. He utilized a dark color scheme for most of his characters and backgrounds to contrast with the bright, bloody carnage. *30 Days of Night* isn't pretty in the traditional sense, but with its grotesqueries comes a strange kind of beauty. Templesmith excels at utilizing both foreground and background, bringing a particular item into focus to let the horror slowly seep into you from the background.

30 Days of Night's focus on shocking imagery and unconventional presentation gives readers hungry for the dreadful and the dark something to sink their meager human teeth into; and, with this complete story being the first of many set in this dark world, it's an all-you-can-eat buffet.

They're watching you.

UZUMAKI

Written by/art by: Junji Ito • Publisher: VIZ Media LLC; Dix Tra edition; 2013

Spirals. Ever moving outward, ever moving inward. Anything can become an object of obsession, and for the town of Kurozo-Chu, spirals are an obsession that turns sinister. Whirlpools, whirlwinds, spiral hair, spiral stairs ... anything you might imagine as a spiral, Junji Ito imagines as a spiral from hell. Protagonists Kirie and Shuichi flit from chapter to chapter barely surviving a barrage of the bizarre, dealing with things like cursed, curly hair, undead jack-in-the-boxes, and man-eating, vortex-headed women.

Ito portrays the grotesque with aplomb—most chapters pay off by ending with some fantastically horrifying visuals, but often it's the subtle little details on mundane things where Ito delivers his most insidious dread. The unsettling line work on objects like snails or charts of the anatomy of an ear make the normal seem abnormal. His human characters fare no better; as they often have gaunt, ominous expressions, with dark and sunken sockets surrounding chalky eyes and pinpoint pupils

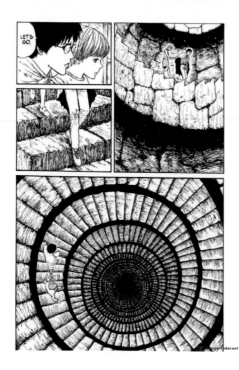

"LATELY I'VE COME TO LOVE THAT PATTERN.
I'M COLLECTING EVERYTHING THAT HAS SPIRALS."
—MR. SAITO

There's no escaping the spirals.

betraying the madness lurking within them.

In *Uzumaki's* supplementary notes, Ito cites H.P. Lovecraft as one of his most formative influences, and that influence is clear throughout this deliciously demented configuration of ink and insanity. Like a Lovecraftian monster, *Uzumaki* isn't about a monster that can be stabbed, or a curse that can be undone, this is a shape, a *concept* as a horrifying, cosmic force that's unknowable, uncaring, and unstoppable.

While many of *Uzumaki's* chapters are self-contained tales of the dark and insane, overall this horror classic ruminates on the destructive power of obsession. Kurozo-Chu's obsession with spirals leads to widespread death and destruction, yet without obsession, *Uzumaki* wouldn't exist, as Ito himself ends the book detailing the obsessions he developed with spirals in order to better write about obsessing over them.

Horror manga artist Junji Ito is an expert on the creeps, a master of the heebie-jeebies, and the mayor-for-life of spookytown. He's authored numerous stories both short and longform, often dealing with the darkest corners of the human psyche with depictions of deranged obsessions and supernatural terrors. Ito crafts grotesque sights in astonishing ways with images that perfectly veer into the uncanny valley of disconcertion. No matter what's happening in his horror stories, there's an air of *wrongness* to everything. The sunken eyes and vacant stares of Ito's characters belie an infinite insanity lurking even in the most seemingly-serene moments. When the crap *really* starts to hit the fan, it's a two-ton truck of feces splattering everywhere, filling your mouth as you scream at the sheer awfulness of it all.

Like much of the best horror, Ito's short stories often come and go without rhyme or reason to the atrocities within. Sometimes there's a moral to be found in the story; others, the only real takeaway is that Junji Ito knows how to make some seriously creepy stuff.

His works have often been adapted to other mediums, with notable entries such as *Tomie*, about a spirit who incites obsession in all who meet her, and the aforementioned *Uzumaki* receiving the full film treatment. Audience reception is generally pretty lukewarm, though, as no CG artist or special effects guru has managed to effectively translate the terrifying essence of Ito's work from page to screen.

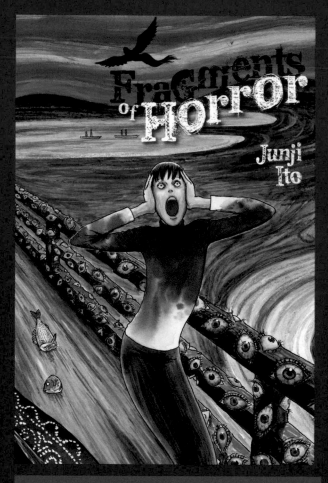

PROMINENT WORKS:
- *Junji Ito's Cat Diary: Yon & Mu* (2015). Unlike most of his work, this is a lighthearted comedic story about the fun and frustrations of owning cats.
- *Gyo: The Death-Stench Creeps* (2015)
- *Fragments of Horror* (2015)
- *Uzumaki Deluxe Edition* (2013)
- *Museum of Terror*, Volumes 1, 2, and 3 (2006)

5 GRAPHIC NOVELS IT WOULD BE IMPOSSIBLE TO ADAPT TO FILM

5. WE3

WHY? The talking, cyborg animals would either be too sad or cutesy, and the radiant (and violent) pseudo-3D panel layouts just couldn't be translated onto the big screen.

4. Killing and Dying

WHY? The style of each story's delivery is as much a part of the story as its overt content, and that style is uniquely tuned to the comics format.

3. The Arrival

WHY? Comics allow readers to linger on individual images as long as needed (or desired) to process them, and film doesn't allow you to take the time to soak in the details of the gorgeous, intricate work of Shaun Tan.

Because of the intricate details of Shaun Tan's artwork that make readers want to linger over it, *The Arrival* would not make for a good movie adaptation.

2. The Acme Novelty Library

WHY? If you've ever seen a page from *The Acme Novelty Library*, you'd know exactly why.

1. Anything by Junji Ito

WHY? Because, as we mentioned before, the guy is such a mad genius, it's freakin' impossible for anyone to translate his madness into motion.

THROUGH THE WOODS

Written by/art by: Emily Carroll • Published by: Margaret K. McElderry Books; 2014

Nyctophobia—the fear of the dark. A mental malady that's infected human beings since before we had the words to describe it. We abhor the unknown; it's uncontrollable and unpredictable, wild and random in its whims. The darkness is the greatest of unknowns, because no matter how long the day is, no matter how many inventions we create to brighten up the night, *it* will be there. Watching. Waiting. Concealing. Thinking. Most of us try to ignore it, desperate to hide from the terror tingling our veins every time we realize we don't know what's out there. Emily Carroll's *Through the Woods* relishes that darkness, and illuminates it just enough to show us that what's waiting in the dark is truly something to be feared.

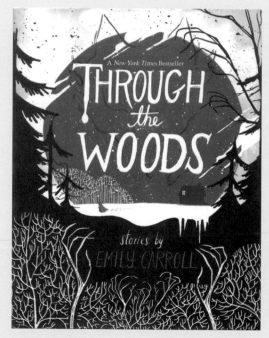

Each of the stories in Carroll's collection are set in centuries past, back before comforts like electric heaters and street lights warded off the cold and the shadows. The five tales each deal with different subjects like the inevitability of death, the pain of guilt, or the siren's call of curiosity. While some horror writers fall into the trap of preaching at their audience through petty tales of horror-infused morality, there are few moralistic comforts to be found in *Through the Woods*. Good person, bad person ... it doesn't matter in the dark.

Carroll's prose and art combine to turn each page into a masterpiece of tension. Her unusual color choices and varied artistic techniques convey a sense of otherworldliness and increasing dread, while her carefully-chosen words each cut with the precision of a coroner's scalpel. Together it all flows in rhythm to crescendo toward each story's chilling conclusion. There's an eerie beauty to *Through the Woods;* Carroll creates images that make even the mundane seem haunting, and grotesquery that horrifies without relying on cheap gore. Many horror stories use simple messages to distract and disquiet audiences without ever lingering too long on the terror. "Be good," coos the other stories, "and you'll be okay." *Through the Woods'* murmur is primal and clear: "Fear the dark, children. Fight it as long as you can. But no matter how long you fight, or where you run, the darkness is always close behind."

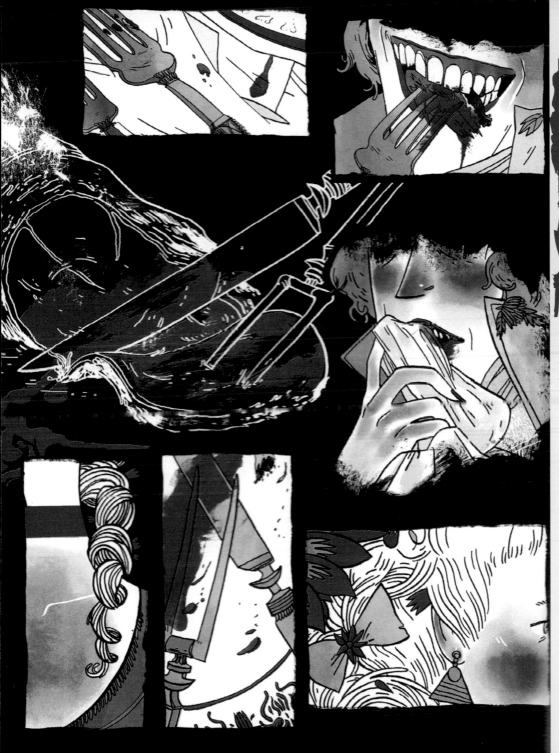

Even a thing as simple as dinner is rendered macabre in Carrol's devilish pages.

SEVERED

Written by: Scott Snyder • Art by: Attila Futaki • Published by: Image Comics; 2013

For those deserted by wayward fathers, the drive to find and understand their would-be, should-be guardians can overwhelm all sense of logic and safety. The need to know our past can drive us, but we shouldn't let it overwhelm the present. In *Severed*, young Jack's need to understand his own past puts him in the sights of an immortal cannibal with a taste for cruelty.

Though most of *Severed* takes place in 1916, Scott Snyder makes use of a Stephen King-ian framing device, bookending the story with the more recent perspective of an old, one-armed man alarmed over a package left by an anonymous visitor. During these flash-forwards, Attila Futaki uses a gentle touch when coloring, giving a sense of the calm, slow pace of yesteryear. The events of 1916 are colored with varied styles, often using rich browns to evoke an old-timey feel. And when things take a turn for the sinister, Futaki goes full-bore in depicting the darkness, using jagged lines, manic facial expressions, and the blackest of blacks to give an overwhelming sense of dread which grows with every page—*Severed* delivers powerful horror. Many lesser horror creators contend themselves to shock audiences with gore, Snyder and Futaki's restrained hands ratchet up the intensity until *Severed* reaches its chilling conclusion.

"ALAN FISHER, FROM TOLEDO," –A MAN WHO IS NEITHER ALAN FISHER, NOR FROM TOLEDO, NOR ACTUALLY A MAN

Jack's adventure is about to take a turn for the worse.

GYO: THE DEATH-STENCH CREEPS

Written by/art by: Junji Ito • Published by: VIZ Media LLC; 2015 (deluxe edition)

There's something insidious about a bad smell. Where's it coming from? What's causing it? How do we get rid of it? Normally, the answers to these questions are simple, things like "the sink," "old cheese," and "throw out that stanky cheese." In *Gyo*, however, dealing with the creeping stench of death is a little more complicated.

Lovers-on-the-rocks Kaori and Tadashi's island vacation gets quickly interrupted by the arrival of a vomit-inducing odor that follows them everywhere. After a bit of poking around, it turns out that the smell is coming from a reeking, mobile fish with crab-like legs protruding from the bottom of its body. This disgusting fish continues hounding the couple even after they end their vacation early and return to their home in the city. Of course, once they get home, like a tidal wave of death things start surging out of control, and suddenly a lone fish with crab legs is the least of their worries. As the story continues and the horror escalates, the death-stench brings with it a disease which infects the populace, turning them into bloated, pustulent

creatures that are both horrifying and pitiable to look at. And then things get *really* out of control.

Master of horror Junji Ito pulls no punches when it comes to depicting the disgusting. Somehow he manages to surpass the limits of the visual medium in his illustrations of this pervasive death-stench; thin, wafting lines invade every page, creating a sense of the invading foulness of evil. Ito crafts a sense of rising dread through his dark-eyed, gangly characters, and increasingly disturbed atmosphere. This building tension always pays off with pages of stomach-churning, eye-averting vileness of the best kind, often spilling out of the comic borders to create a sense of endless, inescapable terror. *Gyo* hints at themes of romantic redemption and the death-smell as a retributive force paying Japan back for the atrocities committed during World War II, but references to these things are fleeting. This book primarily wants to shock you, to nauseate you, to make you feel dizzy with disgust and beckon the contents of your stomach out of its resting place—in the best way possible.

You should worry;
it won't go away.

SuperMutant Magic Academy

JILLIAN TAMAKI

KNOW THY SELFIE:
COMING OF AGE STORIES

////////////////////////

Coming of age, YA, light novels ... however you want to refer to them, these stories center around that universal experience of growing up and moving on, of finding who you are amidst the chaos of an uncertain world, of puttin' on your big boy/girl pants to kick some ass, and of having your big boy/girl pants yanked down in front of everyone because kids are freaking mean.

According to psychologist Erik Erikson, it's during our teenage years that we undergo a stage of psychological development known as *identity versus confusion*; we're taking the first steps toward arriving at our adult destinations, and along the way we have to decide who we want to be once we get there. It's a tense, tough time most of us don't look back on fondly.[32] With that tension, however, comes a delicious potential for *drama*. Writers have known this for years, but the general public only recently locked their teeth into the power of coming of age stories.

The Young Adult genre as we know it originated with S.E. Hinton's *The Outsiders* in 1967. Hinton was only a teenager when she wrote *The Outsiders*

and saw it published; the novel's truthful portrayal of classism, teenage angst, and violence struck a chord with readers and critics alike. At the time, most novels written about teenagers were written for adults, by adults, with a nostalgic tint to them. *The Outsiders* holds no such nostalgia, instead opting for the ugly truth: Being a teenager sucks.

From there we got such notable YA novels as *Bless the Beasts and Children* by Glendon Swarthout and *The Bell Jar* by Sylvia Plath. Like *The Outsiders,* these are dark tales of mental and physical anguish, with teenage protagonists being forced to leave behind the comforts of childhood for the freedom and responsibilities of adulthood.

After a few decades of solid, but often overlooked, Young Adult stories, the *Harry Potter* series arrived to bewitch and ensnare the genre wide open. These eight novels illustrate the primary conceit of the Young Adult genre—the transition between youth and adulthood—over the course of the series. While *Harry Potter and the Sorcerer's Stone*[33] is a mostly gentle affair full of broomsticks and jellybeans, each subsequent novel grows darker and more mature,

---

32 To all current teenagers reading this: good luck! You'll turn out okay, probably! Just do your best! Everyone's rooting for you!

33 Known also as *Harry Potter and the Philosopher's Stone*, or *Harry Potter and the Buttload of Money I'm Going to Make Off of This.*

its contents growing up to match its aging reader base. Thanks to the unprecedented global success of *Harry Potter,* several other major franchises bloomed such as *The Hunger Games* series and that awful one about sparkling vampires that we won't sully this book by naming. These novels helped pave the way for graphic novels to follow suit with similar tales of heartbreak and burgeoning maturity.

Young Adult stories vary wildly in terms of seriousness and subject. The *Scott Pilgrim* series ruminates on finding love as an emerging adult, using comedy and hyperbolic fantasy to make light of its subject matter. *Blankets* takes a more serious look at young love, and *SuperMutant Magic Academy* flits from topic to topic to elucidate the full experience of youth. The common element tying most young adult stories together is that the protagonist's journey and destination are made clear with hindsight; usually our intrepid heroes discover something the audience has known all along, such as *Smile*'s heroine discovering that she's defined by much more than her dental woes, or Scott Pilgrim discovering that he's a lunkhead.

Making the Story: Kill the Freshman

With my own story, *Kill the Freshman*, I tried to create a world that captures the aspects of ongoing competition between teenagers—social, academic, and otherwise. At the Gracewood Academy of Queens and Patriarchs, any student who steals the ID card of another can absorb their strength and smarts, giving them the edge in a world that demands it. The upperclassmen are like gods, armed with the combined strength, speed, and intelligence of all those students they've climbed over to get

where they are. Freshmen, on the other hand, are fresh meat, and with no powers and only each other as allies, they have to adapt quickly to survive.

The premise sounds harsh on paper, but in execution it's more *Dragon Ball Z + Mean Girls* than *Battle Royale + Heathers.* I created this as a fun

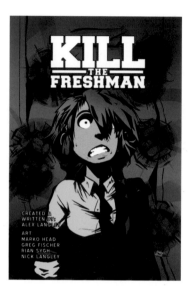

action-adventure story that highlights the often oppressive social structures of high school.

My protagonist, a freshman named Vi, barely manages to survive life at Gracewood until she lucks her way into a friendship with the school's top senior, Allison Meadows. Allison's obsessed with being at the apex of Gracewood's social and academic structure, no matter who she has to crush on her way there. As an audience, we get to watch as these two deuteragonists learn from each other while trying to decide if they would rather conform to Gracewood's brutal standards, or band together with their friends to stay strong in the face of tyranny. To us, the answer to this question is (probably) obvious, but to these heroes, it's not, and the journey they make while trying to find this answer, the complicated allies they gain, and the fearsome foes they battle, are what make it worthwhile.

Making a graphic novel is a long, arduous process

— especially when you're a writer, not an artist. It took many months and countless hours of going over page layouts, rewriting scenes, and studying storytelling to put this mama-jama together. I tried to stay true to some of the most universal elements of the YA genre—themes of dramatic personal transformations, self-understanding, and a journey enriched with hindsight—while breaking away from common tropes where possible to create something funny, action-packed, and insightful. Whether I succeeded in that goal is up for you to decide.

—Alex Langley

With great seniority comes great power.

MS. MARVEL: NO NORMAL/GENERATION WHY

Written by: G. Willow Wilson • Art by: Adrian Alphona
Published by: Marvel; 2014 (No Normal), 2015 (Generation Why)

New superheroes can come and go like the wind. In the '90s, you couldn't ride a Rad Board down the street without stumbling over an edgy, spandex-clad roid-monger claiming to be *this* generation's Batman. While a few of those goobers survived and evolved into actually cool characters, most of them didn't, and generally it's because they were characters with nothing new to say. Every once in a while, however, the big two comics publishers (Marvel and DC) will put out a character who is boldly different from the rest, capturing the voice and perspective of people who don't normally get to see themselves in superheroes. Ms. Marvel's debut story, *No Normal/Generation Why*, gives audiences a hero that's fun, fresh, and damn original.

Like many teenagers, Kamala Khan feels dissatisfied with her looks, hungers to prove herself to the world, and can't stand the way her old-school parents are always trying to tell her what to do. As the shape-shifting Ms. Marvel, she gets the chance to tackle all the obstacles she's dreamed of overcoming, facing her own body image

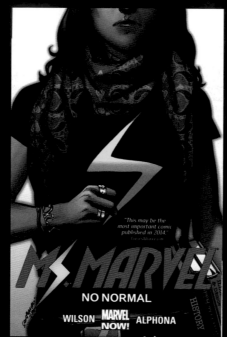

"This may be the most important comic published in 2014."

MS. MARVEL

NO NORMAL

WILSON **MARVEL NOW!** ALPHONA

HISTORY

issues, the tendency for the older generation to disregard the youth, and the everyday ins-and-outs of being a nerdy Muslim gal from New Jersey.

Kamala's Muslim heritage plays a strong part in her story; while her parents are fairly traditional, Kamala constantly wrestles with her desire to adhere to her family's traditions while also finding her own identity (a struggle many kids, especially kids of immigrants, can identify with). Even with a great secondary cast backing her up, Kamala carries this story start to finish, from her early moments as a non-powered teen drooling over forbidden bacon, all the way to her climactic showdown against the clone of Thomas Edison (who has the head of a bird. Like, dude's head is a freaking bird head). She's fast-thinking and fast-talking, always spewing nerdy references to things like *Halo* and *World of Warcraft*, and fangirling out when she gets the chance to meet some of Marvel's biggest heroes (and taking selfies with them).

Adrian Alphona's expressive art uses loose linework and sweeping strokes to evoke a natural, vivacious feel to Kamala's adventures, enhancing her

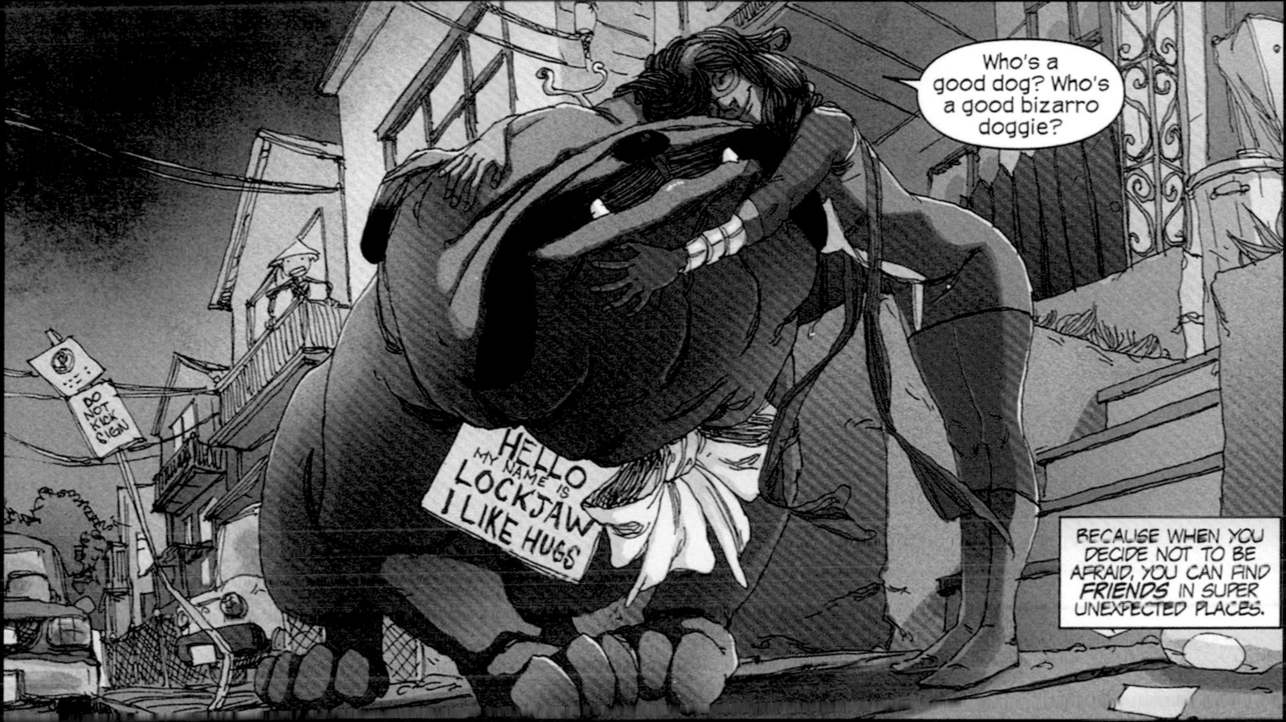
Who's a good dog? Who's a good bizarro doggie?
DO NOT KICK SIGN
HELLO MY NAME IS LOCKJAW I LIKE HUGS
BECAUSE WHEN YOU DECIDE NOT TO BE AFRAID, YOU CAN FIND FRIENDS IN SUPER UNEXPECTED PLACES.

Moon doggies are the *best* doggies.

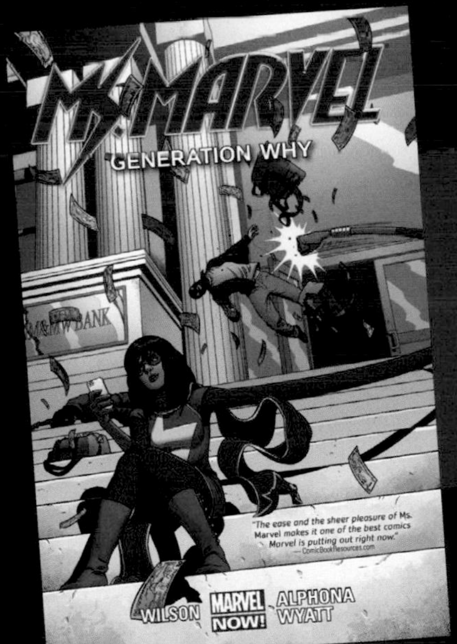
MS. MARVEL
GENERATION WHY
"The ease and the sheer pleasure of Ms. Marvel makes it one of the best comics Marvel is putting out right now."
— ComicBookResources.com
WILSON
MARVEL NOW!
ALPHONA WYATT

"JUST BECAUSE THEY'RE OLD DOESN'T MAKE THEM RIGHT ... THIS IS SAYING OUR GENERATION WILL NEVER MATTER. BUT WE HAVE TO MATTER. IF WE DON'T, THERE'S NO FUTURE WORTH SAVING."
–KAMALA KHAN,
OTHERWISE KNOWN AS MS. MARVEL

Kamala Khan finds her inner (and outer) power.

shape-shifting abilities for maximum effect. Being a teenager often feels like being in a misshapen body that doesn't quite fit you; Kamala's constant shape-changing often leaves her with exaggeratedly huge hands and long, gangly limbs, really showing what it feels like to be a teen. Writer G. Willow Wilson chose Kamala's polymorphing abilities specifically for her character, stating that "I think a lot of these sort of passive abilities are often given to female characters—becoming invisible, using force fields. I wanted her to have something visually exciting, something kinetic ... The idea of making her a shape shifter nicely paralleled her personal journey."[34]

34 Source: herocomplex.latimes.com/comics/ms-marvel-g-willow-wilson-sana-amanat-on-kamalas-transformation/#/0.

SMILE

Written by/art by: Raina Telgemeier • Published by: Graphix; 2010

From the *New York Times* Bestselling Author
Raina Telgemeier

Smile

Dentists—an occupation with one of the highest suicide rates of any profession. It's rare that you'll find anyone who *loves* going to the dentist, but it's a necessary evil for the majority of us if we want to keep our teeth from falling out. If you want to eat that sweet candy, you better plan for a trip to the smile doctor. For Raina Telgemeier, however, it was something far worse than candy that kept placing her back in that chair—it was a childhood accident which smacked out her two front teeth. After that unfortunate childhood incident, Telgemeier channeled her youthful pain into the appropriately-titled *Smile,* a transformative tale about the power (and lack thereof) of appearances.

After Raina knocks her teeth out, she spends the next four to five years going through repeated procedures: casts, extractions, headgear, braces on, then off, then on again, root canals, and retainers equipped with fake teeth.[35] It's like the universe was bored one day and decided to play a cruel joke on Raina, because all of this suffering happens amidst the most awkward phase of development—adolescence. During a time where most people are wracked with insecurity and indecision, trying desperately to figure out what kind of person they

---

35 As someone who's had many teeth problems as well, Telgemeier's descriptions of dental woes ring all too true. One panel features a dentist looking into Raina's mouth and saying the dreaded phrase, "Uh-oh," something those of us with cursed teeth have heard all too often. The only time "uh-oh" is a good thing is when it comes from a cheering crowd reacting to someone dropping it like it's hot on the dance floor. -Katrina

Don't worry, Raina. Vampires are so in right now.

are while their body freaks out in almost every direction, Raina has the added stress of a mouthful of surgery.

Smile's dental woes belie a story about boys, good friends, not-so-good friends, and feelings of inadequacy. Telgemeier's art harkens to Sunday comics; by using simple lines and clean colors, she obtains a cartoonish expressiveness.

Telgemeier crafts a relevant and oddly unique story about the difficulties of growing up while missing your two front teeth. Despite the frequent pain young Raina endures, this is still a fun, uplifting story about overcoming the awkwardness of being a teenager. No matter your age or gender, there's something in here sure to put a smile on anyone's face.

SKIM

Written by: Mariko Tamaki • Art by: Jillian Tamaki • Published by: Groundwood Books; 2008

"I DIDN'T FEEL LIKE SHARING MY LIST, BUT AFTER CLASS MRS. HORNET ASKED IF SHE COULD SEE IT. SO MUCH FOR FEELING COMFORTABLE."
—SKIM

When up-and-coming high school athlete John Reddear kills himself, Keiko "Skim" Cameron's entire high school goes into maximum mourning mode, with worried eyes turning to every potentially troubled student—like Skim herself. Skim has bigger things to worry about than being depressed and killing herself, though, like deciding if she's really into this whole "being a Wiccan" thing or if it's just a phase, whether her best friend Lisa is much of a friend at all, and whether or not she has the hots for her teacher (who may have the hots for her, too?)

Framed as Skim's journal entries during this time of mega-mourning, *Skim* uses an unreliable narrator to entice readers to dig deeper into what's being said versus what's happening on each page. Skim lacks enough experience to fully understand what's going on with herself and those around her; when she and Lisa visit a Wiccan prayer circle, she refers to the bag of "oregano" the adults have. Many of her journal entries describe seemingly-banal moments such as Skim spending the day staying "very still" on the couch, or feelings she's having trouble processing.

Mariko Tamaki smartly contrasts Skim's thoughts with her dialogue and actions, giving the audience insight into Skim's emotional status that she has yet to gain herself. Skim wrestles with self-doubt, often striking through her diary entries to rewrite them as something she thinks is more palatable, yet she never fully admits out loud (or to herself) the difficulties she's having.

Despite most of the story taking place through the lens of a dour teenager's diary, *Skim* keeps momentum thanks to Mariko Tamaki's knack for organic dialogue and Jillian Tamaki's knack for organic art. Each character looks and feels genuine; they say things which are interesting, dumb, stupid, or inaccurate, creating a fully-realized being on each page.

Skim has Wiccan supplies for rituals of every shape and size!

Goddess Statue

Broken Candelabra

(Currently on shawl from Kensington Market)

Chalice

Lavender

Sandalwood

Tea Lights

Book of Spells (Book of Shadows)

Tarot Cards (Must be GIVEN to you or they don't work)

Pen of Arts (Pen for writing spells)

THE SUN

Cloth for holding Tarot

Crystals

☆ STILL MISSING:

• God Statue • Salt Bowl • Wand • Bell • Cauldron
• Athame (Magical Knife) • More Herbs??

• Pentacle ⟶ (I'm supposed to have one on the altar but I only have one and I'm wearing it)

• Incense (not technically allowed because it gives Mom headaches and makes her think I am trying to smoke in the house)

Written by/art by: Svetlana Chmakova •Published by: Yen Press; 2015

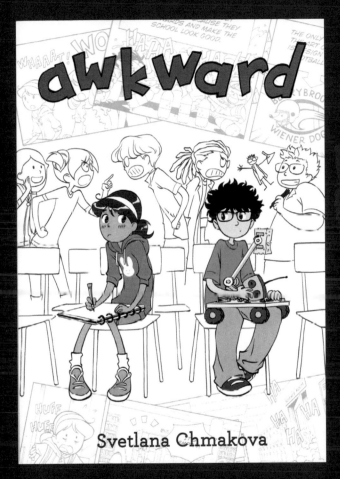

High school, middle school, even elementary school can be really tough on kids—transforming from kid to adult means lots of awkward[36] times, times which aren't helped by the fact that kids, in general, are *mean* little boogers that get stuck in your nose and refuse to get picked out.

> "IT'S MY FIRST DAY AT BERRYBROOK MIDDLE SCHOOL, AND I JUST TRIPPED OVER MY OWN FEET AND DROPPED EVERYTHING. INCLUDING MY DIGNITY." —PENELOPE

Penelope, or Peppi, finds out who these mean boogers are on her first day at her new school as she trips in the hallway, spilling everything all over the floor. The mean kids, with their psychic radars for embarrassing moments, immediately show up and start laughing at her, calling her "nerder girlfriend" when a quiet, "nerdy" boy stops to help her. "Cardinal rule #1 for surviving school," muses Peppi, "don't get noticed by the mean kids." So what does she do? She shoves Jaime, the "nerd," away to prove she doesn't like him, then runs away like a spaz. This comes back to bite her in the butt repeatedly since they go to the same school; every time she sees him it's like a wookie-sized ball of guilt smashing into her chest. Peppi must figure out how to make amends with Jaime without being tormented by the mean

36 Hey! That's the name of the book!

Are mermaids really mammals? News at 11.

kids, all the while trying to save the only part of school she looks forward to everyday—the art club.

Svetlana Chmakova's *Awkward* will charm the pants off of you through its sagacious portrayals of middle school problems, endearingly uncomfortable moments, and life lessons. Chmakova addresses bullying, forgiveness, friendship, and whether or not you can only be interested in one thing[37] in a fun-to-read fashion that forgoes any sappy overtones. Chmakova does a marvelous job of realistically diversifying the cast of characters, giving depth and rich detail to folks who are all-too often excluded in other stories.

---

37 Pro tip: You can be interested in lots of stuff. C'mon, try it! It's fun!

THE SCOTT PILGRIM VERSUS THE WORLD SERIES[38]

Written by/art by: Bryan Lee O'Malley • Published by: Oni Press; 2004-2010

We've all been in that situation where the only way you and your BF/GF can stay together is if you fight and defeat all of their evil exes. It's sadly common (and especially common in Canada), which is why Bryan Lee O'Malley decided to create this six-volume documentary about the phenomenon known as *evil exes*.

Okay, so, like everything in *Scott Pilgrim Versus the World*, we might have been just a little hyperbolic. Scott lives in a wild, exaggerated world where vegans got psychokinetic powers, overprotective fathers slice buses in half to find out if you're worthy of dating their daughters, and video game rules apply to almost everything. If our hero, Scott Pilgrim, hopes to date girl-of-his-dreams Ramona Flowers, he has to duke it out against her seven evil exes, all while trying to find a job, get his band a gig, and deal with the lingering malaise left in his heart from his own evil (and not-so-evil) exes.

On the surface, *Scott Pilgrim Versus the World* is

a romantic action-comedy with a major theme of video games; delve a little deeper, though, and you'll find that this romp ruminates on complicated issues of the heart like the haunting ghosts of past decisions (and indecisions).

O'Malley cites Rumiko Takahashi's *Ranma 1/2* and Naoko Takeuchi's *Sailor Moon* as major influences,[39] and those influences are clear—his simple, often pointed, line work depicts character and action with clarity, and his character designs and expressions skirt the line between traditional Manga and Western comics. O'Malley's a nerd of the most wonderful kind, throwing in constant homages to his favorite things throughout his work. O'Malley also uses big art to add bigger emphasis to emotional beats. When Scott's misguided angel of a high school girlfriend, Knives Chau, tells him she loves him (while *he's* totally into Ramona Flowers), it looks like a freight train of love flying out of her mouth and mowing him down.

Though many of its pages are devoted to wild battles and young adult hijinks, there's a surprisingly

---

38 Which is comprised of six volumes: *Scott Pilgrim's Precious Little Life, Scott Pilgrim Versus the World, Scott Pilgrim & the Infinite Sadness, Scott Pilgrim Gets it Together, Scott Pilgrim Versus the Universe, Scott Pilgrim's Finest Hour.*

---

39 Source: http://manga.about.com/od/mangaartistinterviews/a/Interview-Bryan-Lee-O-Amalley.htm.

Scott Pilgrim and Friends.
Ages: Twenty-ish.
Rating: Awesome.

"OKAY, THIS MIGHT SOUND VAGUE, BUT DO YOU KNOW A GIRL WITH HAIR LIKE THIS?"
—SCOTT PILGRIM

serious side to *Scott Pilgrim Versus the World*.

Baggage is a major theme throughout the story, whether it's emotional baggage formed from relationships that started well and ended badly, or relationships that never had a chance to start in the first place. Scott's friends (like him) all have their own weight to carry, but Scott (like many of us) is too self-absorbed to notice it most of the time.

Scott's an oblivious, occasionally cowardly, dingus, but he, like the rest of his friends, lovers, and nemeses, still manages to be a hilarious slice of real human emotion stuffed into a big-eyed package.

"I don't want to spend my entire life drawing talking heads. It seems like a waste of everyone's time. I do try to cram in more dialogue per page, all the blah, blah, blah. Then when it comes to an action scene or an important emotional beat, I try to open it up a bit and have bigger panels per page." -Bryan Lee O'Malley[40]

---

40 Quote retrieved from: http://www.avclub.com/article/bryan-lee-omalley-14171.

AMERICAN BORN CHINESE

Written by/art by: Gene Luen Yang • Published by: First Second Books; 2006

If you look for Asian characters in Western pop culture, you can probably find quite a few without much trouble. But, if you want to find Asian-American characters who touch upon the special difficulties of being Asian-American, characters who are fully-realized, three-dimensional people with strengths and flaws, good luck. Pop culture has always been notoriously bad at representing non-white people in stories; with *American Born Chinese*, however, we get a look at the struggle of Asian-Americans to find their identity in a culture that places too much emphasis on being white.

This semi-autobiographical tale uses three separate, but interweaving, storylines to chronicle author stand-in Jin Wang's journey from childhood through high school. Paralleling Wang's journey is the ancient tale of the Monkey King searching for acceptance, or, when he can't find it, *power*. Lastly, there's "Everyone Ruvs Chin-Kee," a story about typical (white) high schooler Danny being embarrassed by his visiting cousin, "Chin-Kee," who is written as an over-the-top Asian stereotype. These three seemingly-disparate tales all tie together to fit *American Born Chinese's* common themes of self-loathing, racism, and the conflict of trying not to seem "too Asian." Jin's schoolmates are but one of many factors making him feel ashamed to be Asian, and so he deliberately distances himself from his Asian classmates (and they do the same) by trying to seem as "white" as possible.

"Gene Luen Yang has created that rare article: a youthful tale with something new to say about American youth."
—NEW YORK TIMES BOOK REVIEW

AMERICAN BORN CHINESE

Gene Luen Yang

"I KIND OF FEEL LIKE THAT ALL THE TIME..."
—SUZY

Wei-chen has a way with words.

When Wei-chen, a Taiwanese student, arrives at his school with his giant glasses and shaky command of English, Jin's first thought is "Something about him made me want to beat him up."

In an interview with Yang, writer Kevin Wong referenced understanding this feeling all too well. Wong recounted making fun of a kid who was more 'Asian' than he was; the boy's English wasn't as good, and he would bring traditional Asian foods like sushi to school, so, naturally, the other students made fun of him (because kids are little monsters) and Wong joined in, much to his later shame.[41]

Most people yearn to fit in; *American Born Chinese* provides sharp insight into what it's like to yearn so badly to fit in that you grow to hate anything that reminds you that you might be different.

41 Quote retrieved from: http://kotaku.com/the-realest-comic-about-growing-up-asian-american-and-1724281672.

FRIENDS WITH BOYS

Written by/art by: Faith Erin Hicks • Published by: First Second; 2012

"Why aren't you around any more?"

It's a question many of us ask. Sometimes it's rhetorical, shouted angrily at the universe when our loved ones pass away before their time; others it's the thing we mutter under our breath at friends and family whom we don't connect with like we used to. In *Friends with Boys*, homeschooled Maggie McKay has to deal with the newness of going to high school, with all its crowds and rules and *boys,* her twin brothers constant fighting, her oddball new friends, her vagrant mother, and, naturally, the ghost who keeps following her around.

Faith Erin Hicks' lively characters jump from the page, each with their own distinct struggles and character arcs tying back to this central theme of emotional distance. *Friends with Boys* manages to be funny without being demanding about the humor; if its jokes were people, they'd be the unassuming cool chick off to the side of the party, playing guitar not because she wants an audience, but because she just likes jamming out. Hicks also uses the black-and-white medium to its fullest extent, representing a vibrant range of colors from one end of the chromatic spectrum and the other—rarely have there been so

"I CAN'T GO TO SCHOOL WITH ALL THESE PEOPLE! DID YOU SEE HOW MANY OF THEM THERE ARE?? IT'S LIKE THOSE COMMUTER TRAINS IN JAPAN! THEY KEEP PACKING THE PEOPLE IN, AND SOME GUY AT THE BACK GETS CRUSHED TO DEATH. I COULD DIE!"
—MAGGIE MCKAY, WHO IS HAVING TROUBLE ADJUSTING TO PUBLIC SCHOOL.

It's tough being the only girl in a family full of boys.

many different types of grays, nor have they been used with such skill.

Hicks also touches on what it's like to be a girl surrounded by men; protagonist Maggie is the youngest child in a set of four siblings, all boys other than her, and with her mother having left for parts unknown, that leaves her flying solo on the estrogen front. As a homeschooled kid, she'd never had a girl friend until she meets Lucy, a non-conformist whose words tumble from her mouth before she has a chance to catch them, and the two of them bond over things like Ellen Ripley's badassitude in *Aliens*, or the music of Patti Smith, showing the importance of girls finding other awesome girls to identify with.

There's not always a reason why someone's not around anymore. At least, not a good reason. *Friends with Boys* shows us how we can make peace with emotional distance, either by pushing past it to reclaim a relationship we worried we'd lost, or to let go of that thing we're clutching so tightly it hurts.

Faith Erin Hicks exemplifies how the motto "just do it" can really work out for you. Starting out as an animator, Hicks decided to try her hand at writing and drawing webcomics for fun. That fun resulted in a multi-award winning webcomic, *Demonology 101*. Hicks never let her lack of formal drawing training stop her from doing what she wanted; she kept at her craft until she became proficient enough to get noticed: "Some artists go to comic conventions and do portfolio reviews (I've never done this), other people self-publish mini-comics (I've never done this either), other people go to comic drawing college (haven't done this either). I made lots and lots of webcomics, and eventually made enough comics (and got good enough at drawing) that publishers noticed me. It's weird that it happened that way, but it did!"[42]

After *Demonology*, Hicks published her first graphic novel, *Zombies Calling*, and has continued fine-tuning her skills from there, producing stories noted for their expressive art and sharp, funny writing.

Hicks attributes her success to her patience, estimating that she's drawn more than 2,200 pages of comics, about half of which she described as being "not terribly good." She also studied other artists' work in-depth, particularly focusing on the works of Naoki Urasawa and Jeff Smith.

42 Quote retrieved from: http://www.faitherinhicks.com/about/.

Hicks' *The Adventures of Superhero Girl* smartly parodies typical superhero stories.

PROMINENT WORKS:
- *Demonology 101* (1999-2004)
- *Zombies Calling* (2007)
- *Friends with Boys* (2012)
- *The Adventures of Superhero Girl* (2013)

ROLLER GIRL

Written by/art by: Victoria Jamieson • Published by: Dial Books; 2015

Allison Bechdel (*Fun Home, Dykes to Watch Out For*) created a test, so to speak, to measure the presence of women in works of fiction. Its three simple requirements include that a work must (1) have at least two (named) women (2) who talk to each other (3) about something other than a man. It would appear to be a cinch to pass, but that's not the reality of it. One analysis of 6,387 films show that only 57.6 percent pass all three stipulations and 10.3 percent pass none of them.[43] And that's just film! Novels, both graphic and prose, aren't as well researched, though any avid reader will tell you it's evident just how many literary works also fail this simple test.

Roller Girl by Victoria Jamieson, however, is one work which can proudly proclaim that it obliterates the Bechdel Test like a Power Ranger would a Putty Patroller.

During the summer before starting junior high, twelve-year-old Astrid attends her first roller derby match and ends up face-planting into a puddle of love for this fast and furious sport. She naturally assumes her BFFEAE[44] in the world, Nicole, will share her love and join a roller derby summer camp with her, but Nicole decides to follow her own passion by continuing ballet classes all summer. Thus begins the pilgrimage into uncharted territory for these tweens, making discoveries about who each of them really want to be.

Jamieson fills *Roller Girl* with interesting, multi-faceted women, with a female lead, best friend, nemesis, role model, and whole squad of female Roller Derby-ers depicting various, complex relationships. Astrid's relationship with her mother prevails as an all-too rare image of an exemplary mother-daughter dynamic. Her mom is a force of encouragement who takes her daughter on "evenings of cultural enlightenment" adventures which lead to her discovering roller derby, supports her 100 percent when she wants

---

43 Statistic retrieved from: http://bechdeltest.com/statistics/.

44 Best Friend For Ever And Ever.

to sign up for roller derby classes, and doesn't flip her lid *too* much when Astrid comes home with blue hair. Upon facing the realization that Astrid has lied to her numerous times, she sits down and says, "Tell me about it," ready to act as a guide rather than an obstacle.[45]

Roller Girl's illustrations are in full, bright colors comparable to the work of Raina Telgemeier or Doug TenNapel. The characters, with their round eyes and cute-as-button noses, are charming to look at, and despite targeting a young audience, Jamieson still includes a few hilariously smart fantasy sequences to smash the fourth wall to bits.

With *Roller Girl*, Jamieson crafts a tale of self-discovery enriched with themes of fear—recognizing it, facing it, overcoming it—complete with an incredibly authentic protagonist, dynamic characters and plotlines, and a message we could all benefit from:

"Tougher. Stronger. Fearless."

45 Seriously, just sit and think for a moment about how many stories feature a female character—a mom, a wife, or a girlfriend—whose sole purpose is to temporarily deter the hero from going out to do cool stuff. This is a character seen as a roadblock and a nag instead of a person. "What have you been doing, protagonist?" she asks. "You know those adventures are dangerous. You shouldn't do them." "...Okay," remarks the glum protagonist. Yet the audience knows the hero isn't going to stop doing cool stuff, so all this really does is make us get irritated at the poorly-written woman.

Sometimes, friendship is bringing the right socks.

IN REAL LIFE (IRL)

Written by: Cory Doctorow • Art by: Jen Wang • Published by: First Second; 2014

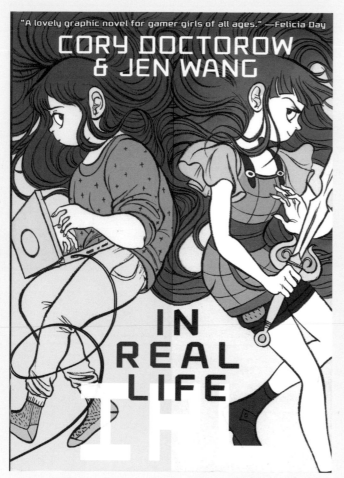

In real life, Anda's your typical teenage nerd, but on Coarsegold Online, she's a badass fighter and hero to the downtrodden. When her guildmate approaches her about a mission to take down a group of gold farmers—players who spend all day collecting currency to sell to other players for real-world money—she jumps at the chance to prove her mettle and take down the bad guys who are ruining her favorite game. During her battles, she meets a gold farmer named Raymond. As it turns out, Raymond's not the money-grubbing monster Anda pictured gold farmers to be, but a battered Chinese boy roughly her age who loves Coarsegold and is working himself sick to make ends meet. Suddenly, Anda sees another side to the gold farmers she assumed were "ruining" her game out of greed, opening her eyes to the many shades of gray in her black-and-white world.

In Real Life (or *IRL*, for short) covers themes of economic disparity, bullying, the blurred lines between our lives online and off, and of women banding together to be remarkable. Jen Wang's expressive art depicts each moment with detail and precision, enhancing the emotional beats and showing the gamey-ness of an MMORPG[46] in graphic novel form. The use of small, cute pixie people to depict the gold farmers highlights their

---

46 Massively-Multiplayer Online Role-Playing Game. That's right, there's no joke here, just a cool, clean definition to delight your brain.

helplessness, and the strong colors of the online world provide visual contrast with the more uniform coloration of the real world.

Tolerance for ambiguity and the capacity to understand situational gradients is one of the last stages of cognitive development as described by psychologist Jean Piaget. As children, things either *are,* or they *are not.* Cookies are good, lies are bad, and we're right. Except that, as adults, we learn of the spaces between either and are, the complexities. Cookies aren't always good for you, little lies are often the only thing holding our society together, and we're not always right.

Anda's growing understanding of the plight of the gold farmers perfectly illustrates this final stage of cognitive evolution. In the beginning of the story she sees them as a blanket "bad thing" in her youthful naiveté, but by story's end, she realizes that the situation with the gold farmers, like most things, is far more complicated than that. *In Real Life* also shows the many ways the internet can be used for social change, whether it's helping strangers to help themselves, or helping a friend to live a better life—virtual or otherwise.

The most important screen in any game.

SOLANIN

Written by/art by: Inio Asano • Published by: VIZ Media LLC; 2008

You're done with high school, done with college, and you've finally got a job that pays above minimum wage. The only problem is ... the job sucks. Or maybe the job doesn't *really* suck, it's just kind of there, eating up so many hours of your increasingly short life, preventing you from going after what you truly desire (or preventing you from even figuring out *what* you truly desire). Like many of us, Meiko Inoue's going through one such quarter-life crisis, and though she doesn't exactly know what she wants out of life, she knows she's not getting it.

Meiko's job is tolerable, paying her well enough to support her and her wannabe-musician boyfriend, Taneda. Taneda, along with their mutual friends, Rip and Kato, eternally struggle to get their band off the ground. *Solanin* is a gentle sort of story, rarely dipping into heavy emotions or high stakes; instead, the stakes are quiet and personal as Meiko and each of her friends try to figure out life in their mid-twenties. Do they stick with the jobs and lovers they don't like that much?

Do they pursue their true passions? Are they even really unhappy with where they are, or do they just think they're supposed to be unhappy?

Inio Asano mixes character-based comedy with infrequent moments of manga-styled surrealism; many of *Solanin's* funniest moments come from the characters themselves, while many more come from unreal moments such as Taneda's Me Summit, a mental argument featuring dozens of Tanedas each representing different aspects of himself. *Solanin* primarily consists of low-key conversations, with clean, emotive facial expressions and highly detailed clothes and objects juxtaposed against oddly out-of-place photo manipulations for backgrounds.

As a slice-of-life story, things are rarely particularly tense in *Solanin*, but the book has plenty of room for Asano to spend time with each character, letting us get to know them and see the uniting quarter-life crisis from each of their perspectives. Stories often skip that awkward, post-school, pre/

"I AM A CREATURE OF A CONSUMER SOCIETY." —MEIKO

Actually, I'm just called Rip.

My name's Rip.

My real name is Jiro Yamada. I'm a clerk at a drugstore.

My ordinary family runs this ordinary drugstore in an ordinary shopping arcade.

To think it's still affecting me today—life is so weird.

I got my nickname after a minor incident in elementary school.

Oh!

R... IP!

HEY, JIRO! A CUSTOMER!

UH, WELCOME...

Rip ponders life, the universe, and the origin of his nickname.

early-career phase of a person's life in favor of other easier to write phases; it's refreshing to see an author willing to cover what is, essentially, a first-world problem, and to do it so well. Were it not for Asano's strong characters and expressive art, *Solanin* would likely fall flat, as very little "happens" in the traditional sense of story, and yet the book is jam-packed with things happening.

Whether we traverse our twenties with a sense of purpose, eyes locked onto our passion, or float around not really sure what we want from life is up to us. Fortunately, at least we have *Solanin* to let us know that we're not alone.

"There's nothing cool about these characters. They're just your average 20-somethings who blend into the backdrop of the city. But the most important messages in our lives don't come from musicians on stage or stars on television. They come from the average people all around you, the ones who are just feet from where you stand. That's what I believe. -Inio Asano[47]

47 *Solanin*, Inio Asano.

BLANKETS

Written by/art by: Craig Thompson • Published by: Top Shelf Productions; 2003

an illustrated novel by
CRAIG THOMPSON

> "SOMETIMES YOU LOOK AT ME
> WITH LONGING ... EVEN THOUGH
> I'M HERE WITH YOU."
> —RAINA

First loves are sometimes wonderful, often confusing, and usually awkward affairs. Somehow, Craig Thompson managed to encapsulate all of these feelings with a tender touch. Despite the isolation, bullying, and brutally fundamentalist Christian upbringing we see young Craig endure, his story still ends up being sweet, wistful, and truthful.

Growing up, Craig Thompson saw himself as flawed and sinful. Every impending conversation or event was a moment of terror spent wondering what he'd done wrong, what sin he'd committed to warrant what he was sure would be a punishment. Compounding this are his issues with a dictatorial father who punished Thompson and his brother by locking them in a dusty, spider-filled closet for the slightest misbehavior. Thompson always blamed himself for the punishments his brother received, and blamed himself even more deeply for an incident wherein a high schooler molested the two of them as children. Thompson felt like a coward for not stopping it when he and his brother were nothing more than victims—but this feeling of cowardice, like most of Thompson's fears and anxieties, he kept to himself.

Eventually, Thompson meets Raina, a free-spirited girl whose parents, while religious, are much nicer and more open-minded than his, and the two of them begin a sweet, innocent romantic affair exploring the earliest stages of love and sexuality. Together they muse on the future, the ever-growing

This is my bedroom....

It's great.

I WANT YOU TO....

Craig tries to deal with being in a *girl's* room.

intensity of their feelings, and more, all with the thoughtful, inexperienced perspectives of people who are still coming into their own.

Thompson makes use of fantastic imagery to compound his feelings on the page, blending word and art to create something greater than the sum of its parts. Jagged shapes show his metaphysical pain, comforting white and soft edges magnify moments of love and serenity, and a blend of real and imagined imagery evoke the truth of each moment. Thompson weighs each panel carefully, distributing them with precision, to build dazzling, honest images that will stir feelings and memories in even the most hardened of readers.

Ultimately, like most first loves, Raina and Craig's tale sputters out rather than climaxing spectacularly, but it's a crucial part of his transition into a well-adjusted adult, unshackled by the painful vestiges of his youth, allowing him to reconnect with his estranged brother and figure out how he can live a happy, healthy life.

DRAMA

Written by/art by: Raina Telgemeier • Published by: Graphix; 2012

The aptly-named *Drama* is full of drama, both of the theatrical kind and the "omg dra-maaaa" variety. Callie, a theater-obsessed seventh grader, finally gets the chance to live her passion by joining the stage crew of her middle school's drama club, and

she pounces on the opportunity. She's determined to make her first play the most unforgettable production the school has ever seen by building a real cannon that shoots confetti; however, she quickly discovers it's not such an easy task, thanks to the constant stream of real-life distractions like friends, boys, and school dances.

Unlike most depictions of thespian antics, *Drama* takes the spotlight off of the actors and puts it on the stage crew, whose jobs are crucial, yet often overlooked, and Raina Telgemeier's bright illustrations give energy to moments of seemingly banal busywork. Telgemeier received a surprising amount of criticism for depicting homosexuality in a middle school book. Laudably, she covers the topic with a sensitive, casual ease that most readers won't think twice about (and those who do may want to take a good, hard look at their reasons why).

Like any good young adult book, *Drama* covers a wide realm of growing pains, which will uncover familiar memories of awkward youth in those old enough to have survived it and provide comforting, understandable examples to those still suffering through the harsh wasteland known as middle school. *Drama's* wholesome, yet accurate, portrayal of the behind-the-scenes drama of drama club will be instantly identifiable to anyone who is/was ever in a school club.

"I GUESS YOU SHOULDN'T FALL IN LOVE WITH EVERY NICE GUY YOU MEET?"
—JESSE

THIS ONE SUMMER

Written by: Mariko Tamaki • Art by: Jillian Tamaki • Published by: First Second; 2014

Growing up, summer days are the most precious of all, cascading into each other in a seemingly endless torrent of time, giving kids the precious freedom to explore and discover. In *This One Summer,* tween Rose contends with her burgeoning transition to teenage/adulthood while lingering in childhood glee.

Rose and her slightly-younger summertime BFF Windy (her parents are hippies) vacation together every summer at Awago Beach. Normally, Windy and Rose are inseparable, showing each other the kind of honesty no one else is qualified to receive. This summer, the age gap is starting to show, and while Windy is still the same ol' Windy, slightly-older Rose has an entire brain's worth of new thoughts to think about. What's up with that boy down at the corner store? Why are her parents fighting so much? Why do teenagers like those R-rated horror movies so much? Seriously, what's up with that boy at the store?

Kids are often privy to secrets they're not meant to hear. Adults often use thinly-coded conversations to speak their true feelings, trusting that children won't be able to decipher the truth. Rose and Windy are just at the cusp of insight; they're young enough to still overhear dire conversations about abortions, depression, and such, but not quite old enough to fully appreciate the severity of such conversations.

> "HEY, LISTEN, KID. DON'T WORRY ABOUT ANY OF THIS STUFF, OKAY? IT'S ALL JUST ADULT JUNK THAT DOESN'T MEAN ANYTHING." —ROSE'S DAD

Windy shows the proper way to eat a gummy foot.

Rose is almost there, but her introspective tendencies and frequent inability to voice (or understand) what she's hearing and feeling puts her at odds with Windy. Rose continually finds herself intrigued by the unkempt, average, and slightly gross boy behind the counter at the Awago video store (a crush Windy both notices and disapproves of). Her crush is the kind of stupid obsession so many of us can remember well. Your thoughts drift to the person at random, your words float toward them regardless of the topic. If a slightly older Rose could talk to the Rose of *This One Summer,* she'd probably tell herself to stop being dumb and snap out of it. But *this* Rose is nearly a teenager and has many more years of stupid mistakes and obsessions ahead of her. Windy, on the other hand, is still fully a kid, and likes it that way.

As we grow older, many of us find ourselves splitting away from our old friends for unexplained reasons. With Rose and Windy, that divide has just begun to form; whether they manage to close the gap or continue drifting away is left to the reader's interpretation.

Jillian Tamaki's writing skillfully portrays her characters as three-dimensional beings on the cusp of maturity, and Mariko Tamaki's art portrays them as three-dimensional beings with rich, wonderful details. Mariko's characters are unornamented, using minimal detail to portray complex bodies and facial expressions. The backgrounds are drop-dead *gorgeous;* Mariko eschewed a traditional black-and-white format for blue-and-white. This

relatively unusual choice gives a softness to scenes of character interactions and brings nature to life with glorious detail. The rocks and trees pop from the page, the sunbeams constrict the pupils to look at, and the deep waters of the Awago Beach seem infinite and full of possibility.

This One Summer deftly examines complicated family dynamics and the lurking difficulties of adolescence with a tone that's light, but never dismissive, and art which enriches every scene with unassuming nuance.

ANYA'S GHOST

Written by/art by: Vera Brosgol • Published by: Square Fish; 2014

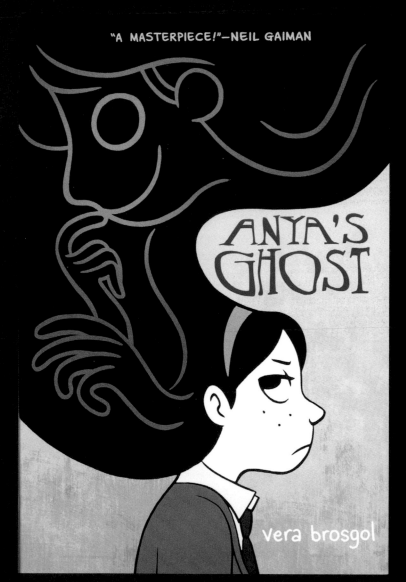

At age four, Anya came to America from Russia with her mother. Since then she's worked hard to seem "more American," paying careful attention to fashion, social trends, her accent, and, above all, to not do anything to betray her overseas origin. As a teenager, Anya desperately wants a thinner body, a better (less sarcastic) best friend, and maybe a boy to make some smoochies with. Instead she gets Emily, a centuries-old ghost trapped at the bottom of a well.

Anya's Ghost cleverly subverts expectations with the relationship between Anya and her phantasmal friend Emily. Early in the story, Emily seems like the ideal pal. She helps Anya ace school, improve her social standing, and dedicates her undead life to building up her BFF. In many ways, she seems typical of the best friend archetype found in most young adult stories, existing only to serve as a foil/hype man for the main character. But over the course of the story, Anya learns of the complex, often superficial truths, to teenage social dynamics. She finds that everyone is so caught up worrying about their own crap that they generally don't think much about what anyone else is going through, and that what people seem like in public and who they really are rarely sync up—like the boy she's had a crush on from afar, who turns out to be a cheating scumbag, or his hot and popular girlfriend who turns out to be an insecure mess, aiding in his infidelity for fear of the social fallout. And while Anya works to become a better person, one who is happier with who she is and what she has, Emily feels betrayed that her best friend would ignore all the hard work she's put in, and things get ugly.

Brosgol smartly ties together themes of empathy and identity with this moderately-supernatural story of teenage angst. Her clean art style gives greater weight to subtleties like facial expression and body language while her strong writing gives her characters a lived-in feel.

Well, ain't this a pickle?

SUPERMUTANT MAGIC ACADEMY

Written by/art by: Jillian Tamaki • Published by: Drawn and Quarterly; 2015

At first glance, *SuperMutant Magic Academy* may not seem to have a story, as each page is a six-panel series depicting some small, often comedic, moments in the lives of the students of the titular school. As you progress through it, however, a narrative begins to emerge of the difficulties of being a teenager. Sure, *SMMA* is a hilarious book, but beneath the humor lies some real truths about the harshness of growing up, bits of introspective wisdom through the inexperienced eyes of teenagers. The students of *SMMA* muse on impermanence, social facades, self-expression, unrequited love, the uncertainty of the futures that loom ever-closer, and why it's important to streak through a fashion show and scream "Fashion is bullshit!" at the audience.

Tamaki uses (mostly) black and white linework to instill life into every panel, and while there tends to be a punchline (of sorts) to each six-panel sequence, there's often more lurking under the surface under subsequent examinations. Tamaki's work is reminiscent of early *Peanuts* strips, back when Charles M. Schultz had a real message to convey about the lonely difficulty of childhood and the almost infinite capacity for cruelty that children have (before he contended himself to merely slap Snoopy's dog face on every manufactured object imaginable and call it a day). Being a teenager is a weird, confusing time, where new adult emotions, thoughts, and feelings are in direct conflict with

This lava is trying to decide whether it just can or just can't even.

lingering childhood idealogies; *SuperMutant Magic Academy* brings that conflict to life with beautiful directness thanks to its fantastic cast of foxgirls, psychics, immortals, chosen ones, and cats wearing tiny hats.

BEHIND THE INK: JILLIAN TAMAKI

Jillian Tamaki got her start as an illustrator and cartoonist, publishing work in *The New Yorker* and *The New York Times*, as well as producing graphic novels. Tamaki often pairs up with her cousin, writer Mariko Tamaki, and together they make an explosively dynamite duo, producing both the award-winning *Skim* and the also-award-winning *This One Summer*. While Tamaki's proven herself as a strong collaborator, she's more than capable of tackling projects alone, as exemplified by her also-award-winning *SuperMutant Magic Academy*.

Tamaki's art training comes from collegiate coursework, studying *Archie* comics, and, interestingly enough, "copying photographs of horses."[48] She has a knack for organic line work on her characters, using simplistic facial features to belie complex emotions, and creating jaw-dropping backgrounds.

Tamaki often receives remarks from fans about her work being feminist due to her primarily featuring women—which shows how skewed many people's perspectives are when they don't think anything about a work featuring almost nothing but men. Tamaki responded to such comments by saying, "…I'm like: 'I guess?' That's just my lens. That's my filter, that's my medium that I exist in, every day. It's not at all subconscious. That's what I'm interested in– female experience … I need to spend less time in the minds of straight men, especially now."[49]

PROMINENT WORKS:
- *Skim* (2008)
- *This One Summer* (2014)
- *SuperMutant Magic Academy* (2015)

48 Quote retrieved from: http://jilliantamaki.com/faq/.
49 Quote retrieved from: http://www.theguardian.com/books/2015/apr/24/jillian-tamaki-comics-graphic-novel-supermutant-magic-academy.

"ONE HIGH SCHOOL KID'S OPINION DOES NOT MAKE YOU UNLOVABLE."
–FRANCES, THE UNSTOPPABLY AVANT-GARDE, SUPERMUTANT MAGIC ACADEMY

CHAPTER 4

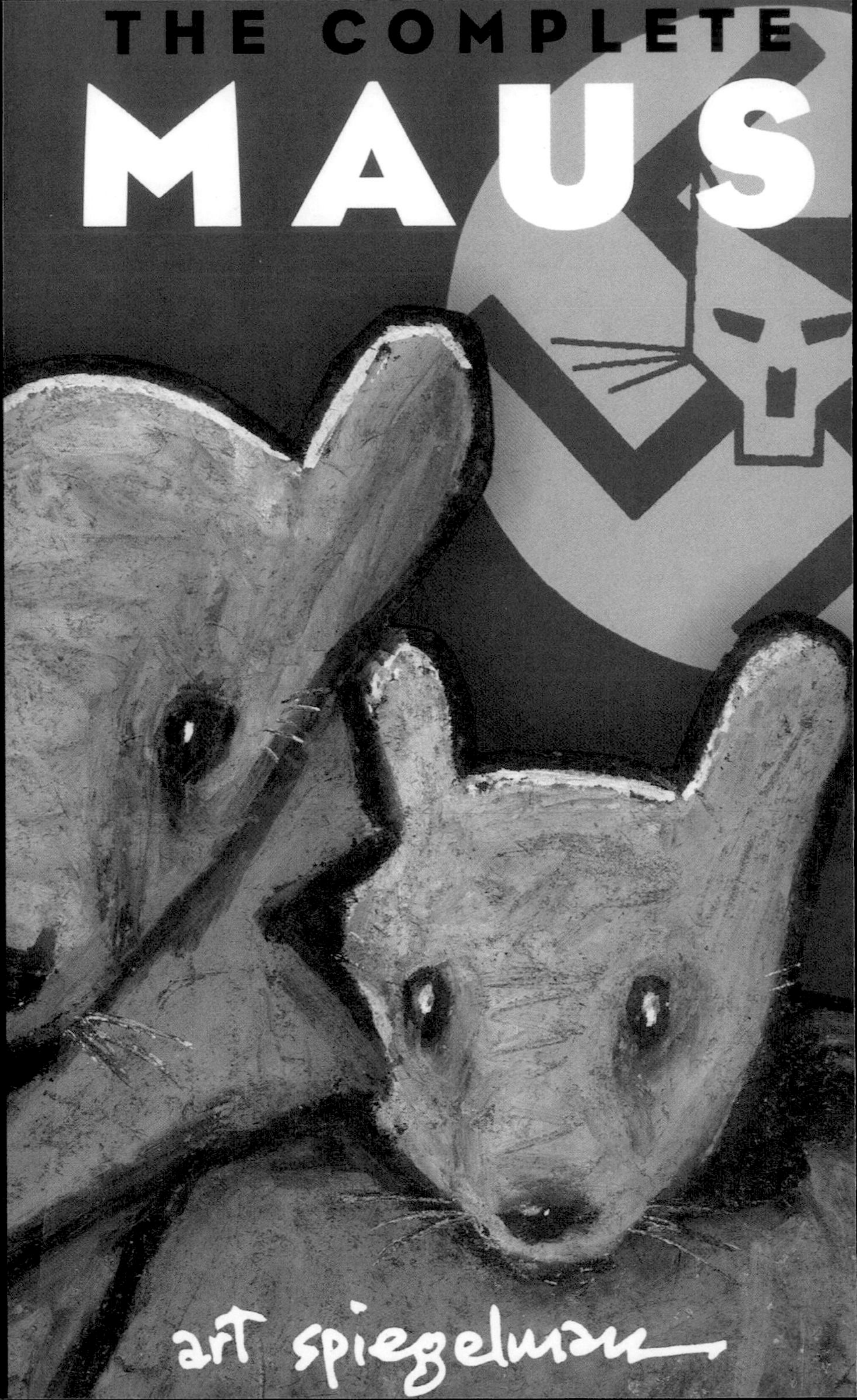
THE COMPLETE
MAUS
art spiegelman

HISTORICAL LITERATURE:
TRUTH AND PAIN, PAIN AND TRUTH

///////////////////////

f you haven't lived through an event, it's difficult to fully understand the truth of that event. Over time, history can become warped, paring away details that don't fit the narrative a particular historian is looking to weave, so things like the emotions felt by those who lived the event, the actions leading up to it, and the repercussions of it, can be forgotten. Historical literature allows an in-depth look at a specific time period and the people who experienced it—their motivations, their struggles, and the near-impossible decisions they had to make. Sometimes these stories **bring truth** in the form of memoirs of a life hard-lived, other times, writers combine real accounts of the past to craft historical fiction, giving a better sense of what was actually happening than any one person's story ever could.[50]

Tales of the Great Depression, World War I and II, and the American Civil Rights Movement are frequent topics of American historical fiction and literature. These moments, while heart-wrenching, make for a compelling read, enticing readers to gain a deeper understanding of past conflicts and sacrifices. A story about a person who grew up with a great family and food on the table makes for a good life, but it doesn't make for a good story.

One admirable aspect of historical literature is the variety of viewpoints offered through them. Textbooks are, in theory, supposed to present a nonpartisan view, yet are often skewed. According to cultural critic Walter Benjamin, "History is written by the victors," [51] meaning it's often the underdogs whose stories are forgotten. Be thankful, then, that we have historical prose and graphic novels to fill in the gaps of some underdogs. John Lewis' first-hand experiences of the Civil Right Movement detailed in *March* is probably different from his parents' experiences, or a Caucasian teenager at the time. Vladek Spiegelman's experience of the Holocaust presented in *Maus* is vastly different from that of a non-Jewish person during World War II.

A good story should bring with it insight. Even if a story is fictional and impossible, if it's a good story, somewhere in there will be a message about the human condition from which audiences can glean understanding. Historical literature is perhaps the most fertile ground for such understanding, as its use of real people and places both delivers a powerful message and garners increased empathy for the real people around you.

---

50 A key difference between historical literature and other forms of literature is the emphasis on era. Jeffrey Brown's *Unlikely*, though set in the 1990s, would roughly be the same story if set today. Raymond Briggs' *When the Wind Blows*, on the other hand, would be a completely different tale if set any time other than the 1980s.

51 Quote retrieved from: https://www.goodreads.com/quotes/97949-history-is-written-by-the-victors.

BAREFOOT GEN

Written by/art by: Keiji Nakazawa • Published by: Last Gasp, 1990; originally published 1973

Indubitably, war produces difficult times, difficulties which can be hard to comprehend from an outsider's perspective. That's part of why *Barefoot Gen* is so important—it reminds and teaches those who haven't been affected by war how unfathomably horrible it is, so that maybe, just maybe, people will try to work toward peace instead.

Barefoot Gen gives us a fictionalized account based on Keiji Nakazawa's experiences as a seven-year-old trying to survive World War II. Rather than recounting history entirely from his own perspective, Nakazawa blends his own memories with that of other WWII survivors. To do so, he created the fictional six-year-old Gen, a loyal, fearless little boy living in Hiroshima. His family endures constant mistreatment and prejudice from others because his father speaks out against the war. Gen bears this cruelty, sticking up for his father, going as far as fighting back and biting off the occasional finger of his abusers. Gen's father taught the boy to "live like wheat," i.e. to continue standing strong in spite of being stomped down, and Gen tries to embrace this morality in the face of increasing adversity.

Nakazawa doesn't shy away from depicting the complicated, flawed perspectives within Japan at the time. It would be all too easy for him (or any writer of historical fiction) to depict his country as a blameless victim and point fingers elsewhere. Instead, Nakazawa attacks war in general by revealing Japan's multidirectional misconduct. The

way high-ranking officials around the globe saved resources for themselves while their people starved, the way Japanese citizens were largely brainwashed by the government into supporting a war that was destroying their country, the stubborn way Japan's leaders refused to give up a losing battle ... Nakazawa holds nothing safe from criticism. When the atomic bomb arrives, he goes full-bore with the details, showing with gruesome style the way the bomb leveled Hiroshima and left its citizens scarred, at best, or melted piles of skin and ash at worst.

The importance of *Barefoot Gen* can't be stressed enough, but know that it's not for the faint of heart. The images of the nuclear bomb aftermath scream unapologetic truth and will haunt you. Nakazawa's expressive imagery and alluring narrative quickly hook in readers, always building toward the tragedy looming harrowingly on the horizon.

It was just another typical school day for Gen until something white fell from the sky.

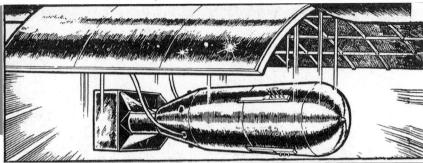

MARCH

Written by: John Lewis and Andrew Aydin • Art by: Nate Powell • Published by: Top Shelf Productions; 2013

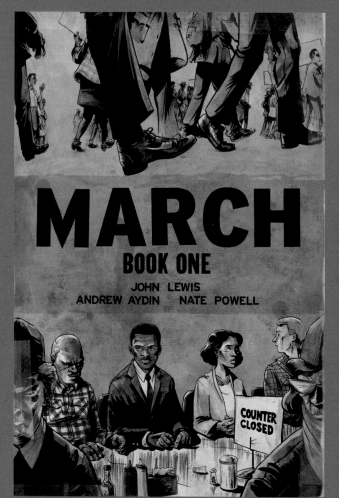

Do you believe in something so hard you're willing to die a very painful death for it? U.S. Congressman John Lewis does; in the three-book series, *March,* this legendary civil rights leader tells of the many brushes with death he had when fighting for equality alongside other American civil rights legends like Martin Luther King, Jr. To younger generations, the Civil Rights Movement may seem like it happened "forever" ago. It's something you watch in a movie or learn about in history books, then move on to the next historical event. It's easy to forget that there are people still alive who lived through this tumultuous time—it wasn't that long ago that African-American people were fighting for desegregation and basic civil liberties.

March covers Lewis' life beginning when he was a child living on a farm in Alabama. Here he would practice giving sermons to a captive audience of chickens, showing that, even from a young age, charisma and wisdom glowed from him like radiation from a three-headed rabbit. The narrative of the past interweaves with present-day Lewis in Washington, D.C., readying for an event—the inauguration of President Barrack Obama. These two contrasting, concurrent narratives merge to create a feeling of reverence for the sacrifices made in the past to produce the brighter future of today.

Lewis, with the help of co-writer Andrew Aydin, provides a first-person account of Lewis' time

FINALLY, JUST AFTER MIDNIGHT, THE MEETING FINISHED.

WE STARTED TO LEAVE,

ONLY TO FIND THAT THOSE SAME TROOPS SUPPOSEDLY SENT TO PROTECT US, NOW **HELD** US INSIDE THE CHURCH.

OUT OF THE WAY--

ALL RIGHT, BACK UP, BACK UP!

GENERAL HENRY GRAHAM OF THE ALABAMA NATIONAL GUARD,

A REAL ESTATE AGENT IN HIS CIVILIAN LIFE,

REFUSED TO ALLOW ANYONE TO LEAVE.

KLOP

STOMP

"WHAT'S THIS HANG-UP ABOUT CLOTHES? GANDHI WRAPPED A RAG AROUND HIS BALLS AND BROUGHT DOWN THE WHOLE BRITISH EMPIRE."
—CIVIL RIGHTS ACTIVIST

Peaceful protest meets the threat of violence.

fighting for everything from the right to vote to being served at a diner; these rich, private narratives give greater depth to the story, leaving most history books seeming flat and cold by comparison. You'd be hard-pressed to find a college or high school history book that details the amount of planning, preparation, and raw discipline that went into events like the restaurant sit-ins. As the protesters were being beaten and ridiculed, they never once reciprocated, operating under the creed which states, "Violence does beget violence, but the opposite is just as true. Fury spends itself pretty quickly when there's no fury facing it."[52]

Lewis was also a pivotal component of getting the Freedom Riders, a group who rode segregated buses in peaceful protest, going. He assisted in running workshops educating interested participants in what to expect along the way while enriching them with teachings from Gandhi, Thoreau, and Emerson. The Riders learned state and federal laws, prepared their living wills, and wrote letters to the President and other influential political figures describing their plan of action (unsurprisingly, they received no response).

Nate Powell really brings this emotional journey to life with his heavy line work and delicate coloring. Despite being a black and white book, *March* depicts many degrees of color in both theme and art. Powell enhances the narrative with evocative illustrations that detonate the sadness, injustice, and violence like an atomic bomb. One panel shows a mother teaching and encouraging her small *child* to gouge a person's eyes out; Powell's illustration of the boy holding his fingers with a look of wild hatred on his face will haunt you long after you turn the page. Despite keeping explicit depictions of violence to a minimum, Powell implies such horror through the facial reactions and body language of the characters. You can feel every adrenaline-soaked second of anger, every moment of limitless agony.

"The fare was paid in blood," says *March,"* "but the Freedom Rides stirred the national consciousness and awoke the hearts and minds of a generation."

March moves with incredible emotion. Schools, libraries, and all places of learning would do well to offer it to those seeking knowledge, as its riveting accounts of the Civil Rights Movement are eye-opening. Just as Lewis and the Freedom Riders awakened a new generation in 1961 with their actions and words, so, too, do Lewis' words continue to ring true.

During the 50th Anniversary of the March on Washington, Lewis summarized his struggles by saying, "Fifty years later, those of us who are committed to the cause of justice need to pace ourselves because our struggle does not last for one day, one week or one year, but it is the struggle of a lifetime, and each generation must do its part. There will be progress, but there will also be setbacks. We must continue to have hope and be steeled in our faith that this nation will one day become a truly multiracial democracy."[53]

52 Aydin and Lewis, *March*.

53 Quote from: http://abcnews.go.com/blogs/politics/2013/08/john-lewis-calls-march-on-washington-50-years-ago-one-of-this-nations-finest-hours/.

MY FRIEND DAHMER

Written by/art by: Derf Backderf • Published by: Harry N. Abrams; 2012

Jeffrey Dahmer—infamous American serial killer convicted of sixteen accounts of murder (he raped, dismembered, and even *ate* some of his victims). He committed his first murder the summer after he graduated from high school in 1978 (age eighteen!) and continued his monstrous rampage until his arrest in 1991. How the hell does someone like this go through school without at least *some* warning signs that he would grow up to become the kind of guy who drills holes in people's heads and pours in acid to try to make sex-slave zombies out of them? Author Derf Backderf's answer is simple: He didn't. The signs were there.

My Friend Dahmer takes us through Dahmer's high school years through the eyes of Backderf, who experienced a side of Dahmer very few ever did—he grew up a few miles down the road from the pre-serial killer and was one of his few "friends" in high school. Backderf conducted diligent research for *My Friend Dahmer;* this isn't just a series of half-formed memories of life in the '70s—he conducted numerous interviews with his classmates/teachers, researching public case files about Dahmer, and interlacing his own interactions to craft an account of Dahmer's high school years leading up to his first murder. What did he find? In the preface, Backderf writes:

"It's my belief that Dahmer didn't have to wind up a monster, that all those people didn't have to die horribly, if only the adults in his life hadn't been so inexplicably, unforgivably, incomprehensibly clueless and/or indifferent. Once Dahmer kills

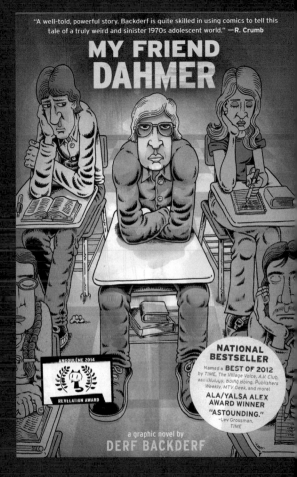

"A well-told, powerful story. Backderf is quite skilled in using comics to tell this tale of a truly weird and sinister 1970s adolescent world." —R. Crumb

MY FRIEND DAHMER

ANGOULÊME 2014
REVELATION AWARD

NATIONAL BESTSELLER
Named a BEST OF 2012 by *TIME, The Village Voice, A.V. Club, io9, Boing Boing, Publishers Weekly, MTV Geek,* and more!
ALA/YALSA ALEX AWARD WINNER
"ASTOUNDING."
-Lev Grossman, *TIME*

a graphic novel by
DERF BACKDERF

however—and I can't stress this enough—my sympathy for him ends."[54]

According to Backderf, his friendship with Dahmer was minimal, but when going through

54 *My Friend Dahmer,* Derf Backderf

the serial killer's recorded prison interviews, he discovers that Dahmer considered their interactions as good times with his friends. *My Friend Dahmer* dives into Dahmer's poor family environment, what a loner he truly was, and the severe bullying he faced. To the audience, the glaring signs of Dahmer's suffering and mental health issues are clear. Even in high school he drank non-stop from the time he woke up to when he went to sleep, mutilated animals (a near-universal habit of budding serial killers), and would frequently miss his classes, but lurk around the school property. Backderf acknowledges the general unease he felt around Dahmer—eventually the young man's cold mannerisms and alcoholism lead to Backderf phasing him out of his life completely. Dahmer desperately needed help, but he was considered so inconsequential that he basically didn't exist to *anyone*. Backderf asks the obvious, but ignored, question, "Where were the damn adults?"

My Friend Dahmer isn't here to campaign for compassion; despite some pitiable moments here and there, Dahmer is depicted as the psychopath he was. Whether or not he was fated to end up as a serial killer is debatable. Regardless, this sordid origin story of one of America's most notorious killers ends with a simple, but necessary message of reaching out to your fellow man and paying attention to those most of society ignores. "Dahmer was a twisted wretch whose depravity was almost beyond comprehension," writes Backderf. "Pity him, but

Dahmer's face remains a stony mask as he mutilates a fish.

KINGS IN DISGUISE & ON THE ROPES

Written by/art by: James Vance and Dan Burr • Published by: Kings in Disguise: Kitchen Sink Press, 1990;
W.W. Norton & Company, 2006 (reprint edition); On the Ropes: W.W Norton; 2015

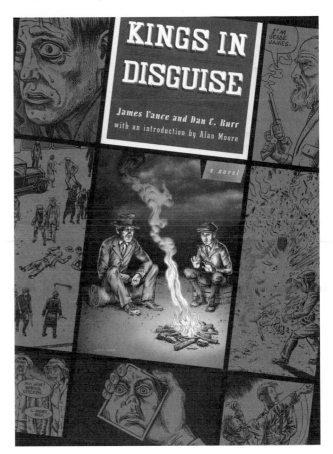

The first half of the twentieth century was no picnic—World War I and its sequel, World War II, affected nearly everyone. The ramifications of these terrible events are long-lasting; in 1944, German troops occupied one part of the Netherlands, cutting off fuel and food trade in an attempt to starve the Dutch people. This event, now known as the Dutch Hunger Winter, left lingering scars on those who lived it—even the in utero babies of women who survived grew up to be more prone to stress and chronic disease.[55]

In the decade prior to the Dutch Hunger Winter, America (and most of the world) suffered a hunger winter of its own, a period of economic downturn, unemployment, and financial hardship known as the Great Depression. *Kings in Disguise* and its sequel, *On the Ropes*, tell the story of Fred Bloch, a young American boy forced into vagrancy by the Great Depression of the United States.

In *Kings in Disguise*, Fred travels America in search of his dad (His goal? To tell him off for being a lazy coward). During his journey he teams up with Sam, the self-described King of Spain (Sam's mental health is an ongoing question throughout *Kings in Disguise*). They travel together, with Fred learning some of the ins-and-outs of being a hobo while Sam tries to protect him from some of the harder truths. *Kings in Disguise*'s characters primarily serve as

viewpoints through which to see the real star of the story, Depression-era America, highlighting the sorts of social and political unrest which grow the loudest when there are empty stomachs behind them. James Vance and Dan Burr intersperse bits of levity throughout (mostly in the form of the charismatic, if

---

55 *The Dutch Hunger Winter and the Developmental Origins of Health and Disease*, Schulz.

Sometimes, a hot can of beans is all you need.

idiosyncratic, Sam), but this is a hard and sobering tale. An early page depicts a schoolgirl passed out at her desk from hunger; when her teacher asks her why she's so fatigued, she explains that it's her brother's turn to eat that day.

Workers, fed up with nonexistent jobs, strike back against the corporations which failed to recompense them for their hard work. In *Kings in Disguise*, Fred and Sam end up in the heart of Detroit's labor strikes. After Fred is forced to leave the injured Sam in the care of the woman who loves him, he continues to fight back on the side of labor workers in *On the Ropes*. Set a few years later, Fred works at a traveling sideshow, using his migratory status to aid the nascent labor union and stay a moving target for the criminal goons trying to unravel their work. *On the Ropes* tells a compelling story of loss, regret, and determination; by centering more on Fred and his sideshow companions, it takes a more focused approach than *Kings in Disguise,* which is more content to wander through its rich setting than to settle its characters in one place long enough to craft a full story there.

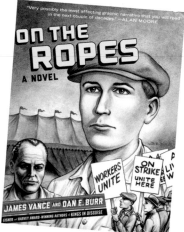

THE COMPLETE MAUS

Written by/art by: Art Spiegelman • Published by: Pantheon, 1996 (25th anniversary edition)

Since the beginning of time, cats and mice have had a clear-cut relationship—cats chase, catch, torture, and eat mice, and mice get the hell away from the cats. In *Maus,* Art Spiegelman uses this well-known relationship as a metaphor for the relationship between the Germans and Jewish people during World War II, shining a spotlight into one of history's darkest moments.

Most of *Maus* tells the tale of how Spiegelman's father survived WWII; wrapping around this tale with a meta-story wherein Artie interviews his estranged father. As a Jewish person in Poland during WWII, Vladek Spiegelman spent years on the run, hiding, starving, spending time in a POW camp, and fighting to survive the brutality of the Auschwitz concentration camp. Vladek is one strong son of a bitch. Where many others fell weak and perished, his iron-clad will allowed him to cling to survival. This iron will served

him well during WWII, but survivor's guilt eats away at Vladek and, by proxy, his son. Vladek feels wracked with survivor's guilt over those lost in the war, and Artie feels a sort of secondhand guilt for *not* having gone through the Holocaust as his parents did. Artie also tries to understand in what ways the Holocaust has shaped who his father has become—impossibly stubborn, extremely frugal, and racist. Spiegelman put the truth first and politeness second with his father's words, leaving every ugly edge and grammatical imperfection in.

Maus' clean black-and-white artwork paints a vivid picture of the strife of WWII. Spiegelman utilizes characters and backgrounds alike to provide metaphorical imagery, shaping walking paths into ominous swastikas, or using both foreground and background images to provide conflicting information. His use of animal faces and tails to

Hard lines denote the harshness of the concentration camp.

depict different groups of people allows readers to quickly identify the arbitrary lines of racial stratification; it also allows readers to identify more easily with people different from themselves, similar to the way that simplistic character art a la *Tintin* allows readers to place themselves in that character's shoes. Without distinctly human identifiers to remind us these characters *aren't* us, we can more easily imagine they *are*.

Racism, guilt, and survival are themes everyone can relate to, and *Maus* delivers these subjects with intricate flair, providing an intimate look into one of humanity's most inhumane ordeals. It was the first comic book to ever win a Pulitzer Prize, establishing graphic novels, in English-speaking countries, as a valid form of art and a legitimate way to address more serious topics.

"*The only way to make any statement about racism was to not make that the subject but to make the subject the history of how racism impacted their lives.*" —Art Spiegelman[56]

Maus highlights the many atrocities of World War II.

56 Quote retrieved from: http://www.pbs.org/pov/inheritance/photo-gallery-art-spiegelman-maus/.

FORGET SORROW: AN ANCESTRAL TALE

Written by/art by: Belle Yang • Published by: W.W Norton & Company; 2011

After college, Belle Yang traveled abroad, then moved back home with her parents in order to get away from an abusive ex-boyfriend-turned stalker. This ex, only referred to as "Rotten Egg" by Yang and her folks, was a dangerous man, in and out of jail due to his obsession over her, and they feared that, should he find Yang, he would kill her. Her days at home were anything but restful, so to keep her mind away from the stress of her stalker, she had her father recount their lengthy family history, drawing comfort and inspiration from the trials and tribulations of her ancestors. While Yang's tale of escape forms the framework for *Forget Sorrow*, ultimately this is an epic, yet personal, account of her family adjusting to the frequent political upheaval in China during the twentieth century.

For anyone unfamiliar with China's political plight, *Forget Sorrow* serves as an insightful look into the treacherous, ever-shifting forces which were at work there in much the same way *Persepolis* highlights the Islamic revolution in Iran. *Forget Sorrow* does, at time, wander perhaps a bit too deeply through Yang's family history, often making pit stops with various distant relatives and leaving it difficult to follow the story's throughline. These pit stops, however, help to paint a fuller, richer picture of her family history, even if they're not always completely relevant to the rest of the book.

Yang uses a flowing art style in *Forget Sorrow*, and ink drifts across the page like the strokes of a paintbrush. This style helps set the tone for

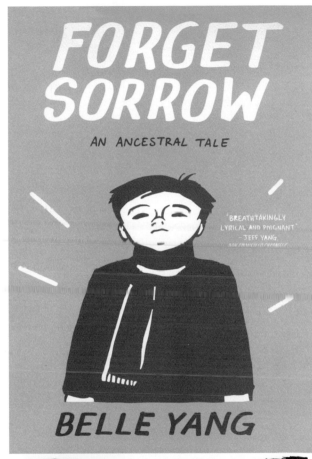

"IF LIFE SPANS A MERE DAY, WHY SPEND IT IN WORRY?"
—BELLE YANG

Yang's art makes the threat of the "Rotten Egg" always looming over the Yang family.

her father's many stories, establishing a feeling of the China of yesteryear.

It takes great courage to tell a story as private as *Forget Sorrow*. Yang's family wasn't always the kindest bunch; many readers will likely find themselves at odds with her family's delicate social dynamics and conservative "Old Chinese" philosophies. *Forget Sorrow* doesn't offer clean answers to life's miseries; there are no climatically cathartic moments here. Rather, Yang offers a perceptive look into the slow, laborious process of adjusting to an ever-shifting world and of healing the wounds of the past.

"If life spans a mere day, why spend it in worry?" -Belle Yang[57]

Four years after graduation, I returned home, seeking protection from an abusive boyfriend, turned stalker.

57 Retrieved from: https://www.goodreads.com/author/show/191431.Belle_Yang.

WHEN THE WIND BLOWS

Written by/art by: Raymond Briggs • Published by: Penguin Books; 1988

Nuclear war isn't (as) imminent at this point in time. In the 1980s, however, many people felt it wasn't just imminent, it was inevitable. Raymond Briggs' *When the Wind Blows* depicts the awful after-effects of humanity's most terrible power with the enchanting, sobering story of retired couple Jim and Hilda Bloggs.

Living in the country with little to worry about, the Bloggs lead simple lives. They survived World War II, so in their minds nothing else could be as bad as that—even a nuclear bomb. When news of an impending nuclear war comes over the radio, Jim and Hilda don't become distraught. They don't even worry. They make the proper preparations, of course, because they're British and it is the "correct thing" to do. As they make these preparations, they continue on talking about life as usual, discussing what they'll do after that pesky nuclear attack is over with.

Jim has an incredibly optimistic attitude; he believes everything will be just *swell* after the bomb. Hilda is more practical, yet she's still primarily concerned with arbitrary niceties like keeping the house clean. The Bloggs' naïve perspectives provide a blatant contrast to the reality unfolding around them; no matter how bad things get, nothing sinks in with these two. Jim unwaveringly believes that his government knows best and will protect them, so the Bloggs follow instructions from pamphlets on how to survive a nuclear attack, doing things such as painting the windows white to deflect the heat, making a lean-to shelter out of doors and pillows, and having a box of sand handy to wash dishes. These ridiculous suggestions are *real* items from real WWII government brochures; author Raymond

"DON'T WORRY, DUCKS. THERE CAN'T BE ANYTHING WRONG WITH YOU. I EXPECT IT'S JUST THE AFTER-EFFECTS OF THE BOMB." – JIM BLOGGS

Jim and Hilda calmly prepare for the nuclear attack as directed by their government.

Briggs presents this "advice" with a proverbial shake of the head, criticizing the government for putting appearances before well-being.

Hilda suggests writing a letter to the Soviet leader, saying: "... will you just leave us in peace you live your life and we'll live ours hope you are well, please don't drop any bombs ..." It's such a childlike, naïve move that readers will want to reach through the panels and pat these two on the head. Briggs' purposeful misspelling and mispronunciation of certain words also adds to Jim and Hilda's sweet ignorance; computers are "commuters," protractor is a "protactor," and terrific is "triffic." It's small touches like these which help deepen your empathy for these two and heighten the anxiety you feel as the story soldiers forward.

If a picture is worth a thousand words, then *When the Wind Blows'* art is a speech so epic it will make your ears bleed. The Bloggs' words and actions are in complete contrast to what's happening around them,

and the art masterfully illustrates this contrast. The earliest pages are bright and cheery, but colors grow darker and more muddled as the story continues and the nuclear bomb's effects are felt, with Jim and Hilda growing paler and less healthy by the page, all the while still talking as if everything is quite all right. Sometimes their ignorance is funny, but in a darkly ironic, guilty-laugh sort of way. It's powerful stuff, brilliantly using the art and dialogue both together and against each other.

Briggs faced significant difficulty in getting *When the Wind Blows* published, as graphic novels were a still-nascent medium at the time.[58] His hard work was well worth it, though, as *When the Wind Blows* continues to be an influential commentary on the dire nature of war, one that's told simply, through the use of a happy, naïve couple who could too easily be any of us.

58 Briggs himself referred to what he did as "strip cartooning," as Art Spiegelman's *Maus* had yet to arrive to help propagate the term "graphic novel" to the general public.

TEN OF THE GREATEST FILM ADAPTATIONS OF GRAPHIC NOVELS[59]

The struggle to adapt source material from one medium to another is always a fascinating thing; sometimes directors and writers just don't get it. They've been handed the thankless task of taking something with an established fanbase (who are ready to get almighty pissed if things don't turn out the way they want them to) and transforming it into something that's roughly the same, but delivered in a different way. And, so, these directors and writers make something which is, at best, mediocre, and at worst a pile of hot roadkill so putrid it makes vultures puke for days. Sometimes, however, the right project ends up in the hands of the right adaptation team, and the result is a new project that embraces the spirit of the original material while applying a new flair to it, bringing it to a new audience who might not have otherwise seen it. Film adaptations of graphic novels are more often in the first group than the second, but when they're done well ... well, they're pretty freakin' awesome.

10. Film: When the Wind Blows (1986)

ADAPTED FROM: *When the Wind Blows* (written by/art by Raymond Briggs)

IT'S THE GREATEST BECAUSE: The animated version of Raymond Briggs' classic work keeps his stark imagery and vivid themes intact, telling the story of the Bloggs couple's oblivious trust in the government in the face of nuclear annihilation. Director Jimmy Murakami blends hand-drawn and stop-motion animation to give the film a distinct visual style, and musical greats like David Bowie contributed to its soundtrack.

9. Film: Sin City (2005)

ADAPTED FROM: *Sin City* (written by/art by Frank Miller)

IT'S THE GREATEST BECAUSE: It captures Frank Miller's neo-noir saga with an incredible black-and-white style unlike any other film at the time. Film critic Roger Ebert said of the film that it "doesn't really tell a story set in time and space. It's a visualization of the pulp noir imagination, uncompromising and extreme. Yes, and brilliant."[60]

8. Film: 300 (2006)

ADAPTED FROM: *300* (written by/art by Frank Miller)

IT'S THE GREATEST BECAUSE: Zack Snyder may not understand how to make a good Superman movie,[61] but he knows how to make a film that's visually appealing, and boy does he understand exaggerated hyper-masculinity. *300* doesn't tell what most would call a smart or dynamic story, but it's still a solid action flick that went on to make a pretty hefty chunk of money.

---

59 These flicks are numbered in no particular order, so save the angry messages ranting at us for putting THIS film ahead of THAT film and how dare we.

60 Quote retrieved from: http://www.rogerebert.com/reviews/sin-city-2005.

61 BOOM! *Man of Steel* sucks! We said it! *mic hurled across room*

7. Film: Captain America: The Winter Soldier (2014)

ADAPTED FROM: *Captain America: The Winter Soldier* (written by Ed Brubaker; art by Steve Epting, Mike Perkins, and Michael Lark)

IT'S THE GREATEST BECAUSE: It's one of the smartest big-budget superhero stories ever told, blending high-powered, super-spy action with a frank discussion of one of the founding conflicts upon which the United States is built: freedom versus security. As government-created security increases, personal freedom decreases. *The Winter Soldier* muses on this theme and more while delivering a spectacle of pulse-pounding action accompanied by a dire, yet heroic, soundtrack.

6. Film: Persepolis (2007)

ADAPTED FROM: *Persepolis* (written by/art by Marjane Satrapi)

IT'S THE GREATEST BECAUSE: It faithfully adapts Satrapi's important, heartfelt story of life in Iran during the Iranian Revolution of the 1980s, using a black-and-white style to keep its themes of hope, despair, oppression, and rebellion universally relatable.

5. Film: Batman Begins (2005)

ADAPTED FROM: *Batman: Year One* (written by Frank Miller; art by David Mazzucchelli)

IT'S THE GREATEST BECAUSE: *Batman Begins* explores themes of post-traumatic growth, corruption, and fear with maturity, treating the character of Batman with a respect and gravitas not found in the smartly campy *Batman '66*, Burton's Burtonesque Bat-films, the uneven *Batman Forever*, or the monstrously bad *Batman & Robin*. *Batman Begins* also lead to the awesome *Dark Knight*, which is a plus ... though it also lead to *The Dark Knight Rises*, which we won't hold against it.

4. Film: X2: X-Men United (2003)

ADAPTED FROM: *God Loves, Man Kills* (written by Chris Claremont; art by Brent Anderson)

IT'S THE GREATEST BECAUSE: It's a complex story that makes use of an astonishing number of beloved characters while still managing to tie back to the core conflict of Marvel's Uncanny team of mutant superheroes: that they're eternally locked in a battle against bigotry, trying to bring peace to a world which despises them.

3. Film: American Splendor (2003)

ADAPTED FROM: *American Splendor* (written by Harvey Pekar; art by Robert Crumb, Gary Drumm, Frank Stack)

IT'S THE GREATEST BECAUSE: It uses an unconventional film style to convey the spirit of Pekar's *American Splendor* series of

autobiographical graphic novels and comics, which are often funny, often sad, and always insightful.

2. Film: Scott Pilgrim vs. the World (2010)

ADAPTED FROM: *The Scott Pilgrim* six-volume series (written by/art by Bryan Lee O'Malley)

IT'S THE GREATEST BECAUSE: No director was as qualified to bring O'Malley's high-energy, comedic action-adventure series to life as Edgar Wright, whose flair for intricate, visual storytelling is unmatched. Somehow, Wright manages to pack six volumes worth of story into a lightning-fast film, staying loyal to the source material while adapting it in ways which use the medium of film to its advantage. While not a theatrical success, *Scott Pilgrim vs. the World* went on to find success as a cult classic, continuing to gather new fans who discover this gem over time.

1. Film: Akira (1988)

ADAPTED FROM: *Akira*, the six-volume Manga series (written by/art by Katsuhiro Otomo)

IT'S THE GREATEST BECAUSE: The anime is better known in most circles than the book—which is impressive in its own right—it's based on. *Akira*'s cyberpunk, dystopic, science-fiction setting delves into the corruptive abilities of absolute power and the increasingly isolative nature of our increasingly cybernetic world, both ideas which have only become more relevant since its release. Also, while many anime series and films will cut corners to reduce the cost of animation, no expense was spared for *Akira*—its environments are highly detailed, its characters fluidly animated, and its visual style is

unforgettable. Countless modern animators look to *Akira* as the golden standard of animated storytelling, citing it as the reason they got into animation. For example, there's a famous, visually distinctive shot of one character sliding his motorcycle to the side that's been recreated over and over as a tribute to *Akira*, with shows like *Batman: The Animated Series*, *Teenage Mutant Ninja Turtles*, *Adventure Time*, and countless others all crafting their own takes on the iconic shot.

EPILEPTIC

Written by/art by: David B.
Published by: Originally published in French by L'Association, 1996-2003; Pantheon, 1996 (reprint edition)

David B. depicts his brother's increasingly severe epilepsy using fantastic illustrations.

Having a chronically ill child puts tremendous strain on a family. In the past, this strain was even worse than it is today, as primitive health care and lack of public knowledge brought increased difficulty, cost, and stigma. *Epileptic* recalls author/artist David B.'s life growing up with an epileptic brother, using fantastical art to depict the ever-building turmoil of the condition.

Much of *Epileptic* takes place during the 1960s. David's family, desperate to treat his increasingly-sick brother, Jean-Christophe, tries everything, even going so far as to join a commune (or a cult, depending on your perspective) focused on alternative medicine. As Jean-Christophe gets older, he gets worse, both physically and mentally; over the course of the book, he transforms from a spindly, bright-eyed kid to a bulbous, slack-jawed adult, rendered monstrous by his medication and lifestyle. *Epileptic* is an agonizing read but uses compelling artistic choices to highlight the misery and confusion of chronic illness.

UNTERZAKHN

Written by/art by: Leela Corman • Published by: Schocken; 2012

If you're on the fence about having children, *Unterzakhn* could be the thing to firmly knock you over into the "Yard of No Babies." In this turn-of-the-twentieth-century tale, twin sisters Esther and Fanya lead lives that manage to be completely different, yet largely defined by the same thing: sex.

New York's Lower East Side wasn't the easiest place to live back then—between poverty, bigotry, and archaic, middlingly effective medical treatments, living long enough to see retirement was a dream for most. As little girls, Fanya and Esther approached this harsh world very differently. Fanya was always the smarter,

more idealistic one, taking to academic pursuits like reading and often letting her curiosity get the better of her. Conversely, Esther learned to turn inward, relying mostly on herself, and growing hard in the face of a world that wants to take advantage of her. Ultimately, Fanya becomes an assistant to Bronia the Cuziernerka (a back-alley obstetrician/gynecologist) while Esther—later known as "Delilah"—becomes a dancer-turned-prostitute-turned theater star, one whose line of starry-eyed lovers stretched across the Hudson river.

Leela Corman's art seems flawed, almost crude, yet works with *Unterzakhn's* story to create an image

The sisters' first taste of their mother's hypocrisy.

"SEXUAL SLAVERY AWAITS THE WOMAN WHO ALLOWS A MAN TO ENTRAP HER, EITHER IN MARRIAGE OR IN QUICK AND UGLY GUTTER UNION."
—BRONIA THE CUZIERNERKA

of city life in all its malformed, uneven details, and depicts sex with such ugliness that any potential erotic value is shredded away, replaced with the meaning and purpose behind each coupling of nude bodies. Corman's knowledge of turn-of-the-century culture as well as the Yiddish language gives a reality to her dialogue; these characters, with their imperfections and often contradictory behaviors and ideas, feel like human beings who really lived.

Unterzakhn seems to be largely anti-marriage and anti-children; Fanya adopts the principles of her mentor, abhorring marriage and children alike, even going so far as to destroy her career to help educate women about their reproductive options (options educators continue fighting to inform women about to this day). The twins' father is a gentle soul, trapped in a terrible marriage with a revolting, hypocrite of a wife who cheats on him constantly while berating her daughters for having even indirect curiosity about sex. *Unterzakhn*'s driving throughline is the contrast between the twin sisters' ever-evolving ideologies. In a world as harsh as the one they live in, Fanya's principled approach to life is ultimately self-destructive, while Esther's ability to armor herself emotionally is how she's able to flourish and survive in spite of those who would take advantage of her.

STITCHES

Written by/art by: David Small
Published by: W.W. Norton & Company; 2009

As technology advances, so, too, does medical knowledge. We look back at past medical practices with a shake of the head, admonishing past physicians for doing things like drilling holes in the heads of schizophrenic patients, using vibrators to give women orgasms as treatment for their "hysteria," or putting leeches on people for damn near everything.[62] It must have been incredibly difficult to live in such comparatively primitive times—a difficulty David Small, born in 1945, knows all-too-well, and has chronicled in his memoir, *Stitches*.

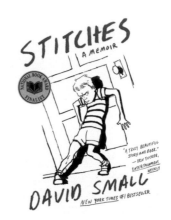

David was born a "sickly child," with numerous medical issues including lung and sinus problems. His father, being a radiologist, treated him according to the medical recommendations at the time—by flooding his body with radiation. Not only did David not get superpowers, he actually got sicker than he was before thanks to the not-so-nice side effects

---

62 All of these are true, by the way, even the hysteria thing.

of prolonged radiation exposure. While battling his medical issues (and poor medical treatment) David rages against his taciturn, heedless, emotionally distant parents, his abusive grandmother, and the loss of his voice.

The theme of silence echoes throughout *Stitches*, amplified by its numerous silent sequences bereft of dialogue or sound effects. Small's art is alive with vivid facial expressions that will tell you everything the adults in David's life weren't telling him, as well as illustrate the balled-up pain he felt as a young man. Small excels at fluid, realistic movements, depicting body language in ways that are accurate, yet often overlooked. When most artists draw a character sitting in a chair, they'll have some variation, but mostly stick to the rigid concept of "sitting." Small, on the other hand, might depict the character slouched down low, with one leg propped up and an arm over their head.

Small stunningly articulates his devastating childhood while managing to end his memoir on an uplifting note. *Stitches* will leave you thankful to live in the era you do while leaving you wondering what we're doing today that future humans will look back with a shake of their future-heads.

"A CRUSTED BLACK TRACK OF STITCHES, MY SMOOTH YOUNG THROAT SLASHED AND LACED BACK UP LIKE A BLOODY BOOT."
—DAVID, WHO IS NOT HAVING A GOOD YEAR

It takes the attention of a dear friend to notice the growth on David's neck before he gets any help.

THE CONTRACT WITH GOD TRILOGY

Written by/art by: Will Eisner • Published by: W. W Norton & Company, 2005

In 1978, comic book artist/writer Will Eisner could find no publisher willing to risk time and money on his experimental art project—a collection of three sequential art stories he tentatively referred to as a graphic novel. He kept trying, however, until he found a publisher with the vision to realize what a groundbreaking concept he had, and, as a result, what was arguably the first graphic novel came to print.[63]

Like the meager inhabitants of Dropsie Avenue, *The Contract with God Trilogy*'s stories are explorative looks into a metropolitan life of poverty. It opens with Frimme Hersh, a formerly pious man who curses God for taking his daughter well before her time—no doubt stemming from Eisner's frustrations over the untimely death of his own sixteen-year-old daughter.[64] Hersh grows to become a selfish and successful real estate tycoon who dies angry and alone. *The Street Singer* shows us that everyone is just looking to take something for themselves. *The Enchanted Prince* uses swirling art to highlight the torment of a damaged mind. Themes of domestic abuse, misogyny, anti-intellectualism, greed, and the conflict between cultural assimilation and cultural heritage permeate every story. Dropsie Avenue's inhabitants desperately crave freedom from poverty and being controlled, regardless of who they hurt in the process, and, save for a select few

altruistic characters (such as Eisner's thinly-veiled self-insert, Cookalein), they're mostly deplorable, yet multi-faceted, human beings.

Often foregoing traditional boxed outlines for his panels, most of *The Contract with God Trilogy*'s panels are large, sprawling images without borders, giving copious amounts of room for large facial expressions and detailed backgrounds. Eisner wastes no lines, utilizing just a few thin strokes to depict complex emotions, or cascading, straight rays to enhance the shadows and mood of a scene.

---

63 Although which work actually qualifies as the true "first" graphic novel is a topic which is hotly debated between comic book historians and angry nerds to this day.

64 From *Krakow to Krypton: Jews and Comic Books* by Arie Kaplan.

IF GOD REQUIRES THAT MEN HONOR THEIR AGREEMENTS...

...THEN IS NOT GOD, ALSO, SO OBLIGATED ??

Frimme Hersh shouts back at the cold universe.

The Contract with God Trilogy isn't a collection of stories about community, but communal suffering. Eisner himself describes the work as a "graphic witness reporting on life, death, heartbreak, and the never-ending struggle to prevail ... or at least to survive."[65] It's a hard, often heart-breaking, work to read, but in spite of some questionable elements (such as Eisner's negative and stereotypical depiction of women), it's a seminal work, filled with gorgeous art and bold story choices.

---

65 *The Contract with God Trilogy*, Will Eisner.

BEHIND THE INK: WILL EISNER

Born in 1917 to an artistically minded, Hungarian immigrant father and a self-sufficient Jewish-American mother, Will Eisner found himself irrevocably drawn to the arts. In spite of his tall, athletic frame, Eisner eschewed sports for pulp magazines and avant-garde expressions of human creativity. He quickly found his way into the then-nubile comics industry, producing comics for the short-lived "Wow, What a Magazine!" before eventually creating the newspaper adventure comic *The Spirit*, a noir-flavored superhero story. *The Spirit*, much like *The Contract with God Trilogy* and the rest of Eisner's impressive bibliography, employed groundbreaking visual techniques in its storytelling. It often blended its title into the background (or foreground) of the comic in distinctive ways (a technique often referred to as "architexture"), or creating words using their onomatopoeias.

> PROMINENT WORKS:
> • *The Spirit (1940)*
> • *A Contract with God (1978)*
> • *Comics & Sequential Art (1985)*
> • *To the Heart of the Storm (1991)*

Throughout his decades-long career, Eisner continued to innovate in the medium he helped solidify. Despite a few storytelling choices which have become increasingly questionable over time (such as some of his depictions of women and African-Americans), his influence is still felt today. Comic artists, writers, and creators such as Bill Sienkiewicz, Neil Gaiman, Frank Miller, Denny O'Neil, Dave Sim, Mike Mignola, Alan Moore, Ty Templeton, Jack Kirby, and more[66] all cite the impact and influence Eisner had on them as creators. To honor his contributions to the field, The Will Eisner Comic Industry Award (otherwise known as The Eisners) were created in 1988 as a yearly awards ceremony to honor the best and greatest comics of that year. To this day, many consider winning an Eisner to be the highest honor a work of sequential art can achieve.

66 *Comic Book Artist Volume 2* # 6 by Jon B. Cooke.

STUCK RUBBER BABY

Written/art by: Howard Cruse • **Published by:** Paradox Press, 1995; Vertigo, 2010

People often wax poetic about the "good ol' days," some nonexistent era where the air was cleaner, folks were nicer, and everything was just better than it is today, with those darn kids and their dang technology. Well, anyone going on about the good ol' days is probably white, male, and straight, because, in the past, if you had the luck to be non-white, non-male, or non-straight, the "good ol' days" were about as rotten as they come.

In *Stuck Rubber Baby*, Toland Polk suffers through the terrible ol' days of the Civil Rights Movement. Racial tensions are high, homophobia is rampant, and it's a tough time to be a closeted gay man with progressive ideas and black friends. Though *Stuck Rubber Baby* isn't autobiographical, Cruse's tale reads like one, filled with lived-in details and energetic characters who flit in and out of the story the way real-life people do. As Polk comes of age, he finds himself confronted with new ideas about homosexuality and racial equality while struggling to expand his worldview. Polk's no bigot, but he's been raised in such a cloyingly bigoted environment that he has to work his ass off to shake it. And, as a gay man very much in denial about his own sexuality, Polk clings to "dreams of straightedness," pursuing what he thinks he should be pursuing: heterosexuality. Polk's struggle will likely ring true with anyone who's struggled with their sexuality. While Polk privately confronts (and ignores) his personal demons, publicly he and his friends are

"A STRANGE AND WONDERFUL GRAPHIC COMING-OF-AGE NOVEL." — *VILLAGE VOIC*

Stuck Rubber Baby

A NOVEL

Howard Cruse
Introduction by Tony Kushner

at the front lines of the Civil Rights Movement, standing up against bigotry while they try to keep some semblance of normalcy to their lives. The days of confronting racism and battling for liberty definitely weren't good, nor were they as old as we might hope, but they definitely make for good reading.

Stuck Rubber Baby shows the good times and the bad during the fight for civil rights.

PALESTINE

Written by/art by: Joe Sacco • Published by: Fantagraphics; 2001

For decades, Palestinians and Israelis have disputed the rightful ownership of Israel, resulting in a never-ending war leaving most of the civilians scarred and poverty-stricken or dead. Compelled by the history and ongoing hostilities, Joe Sacco took a trip to discover the Palestinians' side of the story—a journey which he illustrates in *Palestine*. In the special edition of the graphic novel, Sacco writes some reflections about his trip and completed work, explaining why he focused on Palestinian's point of view: "My contention was and remains that the Israeli government's point of view is very well represented in the mainstream American media and is trumpeted loudly, even competitively, by almost every person holding an important elected office in the United States."

Sacco spent a few months traveling around the Occupied Territories in 1991 and 1992, interviewing everyone he could. Once the Palestinian people realized Sacco was an American journalist, they flocked to him. They'd long since lost hope in their leaders and looked to the press to chronicle their plights. Civilians recounted the abuse from Israeli soldiers, showing off their gunshot scars, broken bones, and naming family members who perished in the fight; one photographer told Sacco he'd been surrounded by violence and uprisings for so long, he'd become bored with the whole thing. *Bored* of it.

Palestine represents individuals' history, not generalizations of a group. It is, at times, a difficult read due to the numerous pages filled with images

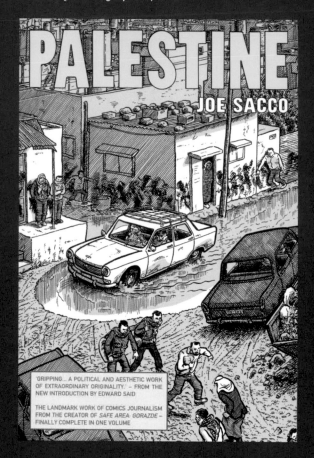

of oppression, aggression, death, and poverty, but it gives voice to a group of people too often ignored. Sacco is the first to admit that *Palestine* is a subjective piece; he comments, "My idea was not to present an objective book, but an honest one." He carefully lets the interviewees form the narrative, making it so that any embellishments and political

The misery of the Palestinian/Israeli conflict affects all.

views don't come from Sacco himself, but the people living it, keeping the focus on the Palestinian people while occasionally interlacing some of his own interactions and perceptions.

Palestine's unusual layout presents its story with widely varied panel usage on every page, sometimes slanting images for dramatic impact, or reducing the number of panels to create increased feelings of isolation or despair. As you progress through *Palestine,* you'll likely notice a distinct increase in the quality of Sacco's art and panel placement; as he progressed through the project, he grew more experienced with the medium, but left early pages intact in the interest of honesty. Most of Sacco's art replicates photos actually taken by him, with supplementary materials providing side-by-side comparisons of the panels with the real photographs.

Sacco also explores the perception of peace with the interviewees. Despite all the suffering, several of the Palestinians interviewed proclaim that no matter what laws come about, they'll fight for the land that was taken from them. One kid honestly admits that if he comes across Israeli soldiers in the street, he will fight instead of continuing on to school. A quote from an Israeli person Sacco interviewed neatly summarized the problem: "Ultimately, I don't think peace is about whether there should be one state or two. Of course that issue is important, but what is the point of two racist states or one racist state...or one racist state dominating another? The point is whether the two peoples can live side by side as equals."

THE SILENCE OF OUR FRIENDS

Written by: Mark Long and Jim Demonakos • Art by: Nate Powell • Published by: First Second; 2012

MARK LONG   JIM DEMONAKOS   NATE POWELL

THE SILENCE OF OUR FRIENDS

THE CIVIL RIGHTS STRUGGLE WAS NEVER BLACK AND WHITE.

"WE PROTESTED BECAUSE WE ARE DETERMINED TO BE MEN—AND NOT LIVE LIKE WE ARE FORCED TO LIVE."
–LARRY, CIVIL RIGHTS LOBBYIST

Tumultuous rubble litters the road leading here from the past. Most of these roads were built with the blood of those fighting for change. Mark Long, Jim Demonakos, and Nate Powell bring to life a moment which helped build this road to change in *The Silence of Our Friends*."[67]

Long draws from his experiences living in Houston, Texas in the 1960s to create this graphic novel. In it, he takes us through the TSU Five Incident, a tragic event in which five black Texas Southern University students were wrongfully accused of killing a police officer in Houston in 1968. The protagonist, modeled after Long's father, Jack, is a television reporter tasked with reporting race issues. While covering a story, Jack meets Larry, a civil rights activist lobbying for the right of the Student Nonviolent Coordinating Committee (SNCC) to be able to meet on TSU's campus. Larry and Jack strike up a rare friendship, crossing racial boundaries in one of the United States' most charged social climates.

Long and Demonakos provide a ground-level look at the time, at the ugliness of otherization, the brutal depths of hatred, and the bravery it takes to stand against friend and foe alike. *The Silence of Our Friends* uses sound and silence to craft a powerfully moving story that will give readers insight into the battle for equality which raged in the past (and

67 The title stems from Dr. Martin Luther King, Jr., who once famously said, "In the end, we will remember not the words of our enemies, but the silence of our friends."

Compassion in the face of adversity.

continues to be fought today, more than fifty years later). Long and Demonakos are honest about the negativity of the past while still managing to find positivity. On one page, Black and White children meet for the first time, taking a few moments to feel each others' hair before quickly forgetting about any differences between them and playing a game together. It's a salient lesson many adults would do well to learn from.

"What we have striven to create is a story that offers access to a particular moment in time, both for those who lived it and those who are just discovering it." -Mark Long[68]

68 Mark Long, *The Silence of Our Friends*.

A PEOPLE'S HISTORY OF AMERICAN EMPIRE

Written by: Howard Zinn and Paul Buhle • Art by: Mike Konopacki • Published by: Metropolitan Books; 2008

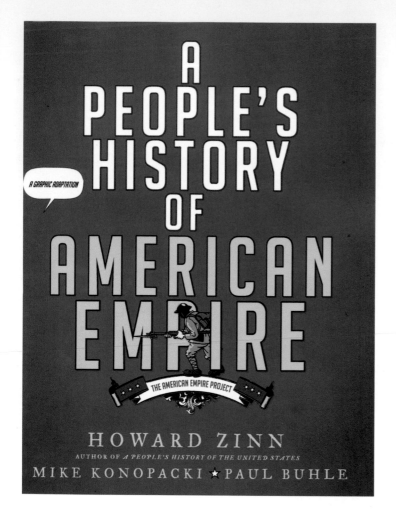

American historian and social activist Howard Zinn wrote over twenty historical chronicles over the course of his life. As a self-proclaimed part anarchist, part socialist, "maybe a democratic socialist,"[69] Zinn doesn't even try to present an unbiased view of American history; his point behind *A People's History of American Empire* is to illuminate some all-too-often ignored truths with a thoroughly researched,[70] thoroughly anti-war account of America's more atrociously Anglocentric moments.

A People's History of American Empire opens with a prologue of Zinn at his computer writing an article reacting to the events of September 11, 2001, and the government's response. It then jumps to Zinn speaking at an anti-war rally, which frames the rest of the graphic novel by illustrating each event as he discusses it. First, he recounts the Wounded Knee Massacre of 1890, then moves

69 Quote retrieved from: http://flag.blackened.net/ias/13zinn.htm.

70 Zinn's work has often drawn the ire of hardcore conservative figures. One such figure, former Indiana Governor Mitch Daniels, blasted Zinn after he passed with the statement that: "[*A People's History of the United States*] is a truly execrable, anti-factual piece of disinformation that misstates American history on every page. Can someone assure me that it is not in use anywhere in Indiana? If it is, how do we get rid of it before more young people are force-fed a totally false version of our history?" Hmm...totally false, or does it just present a side of America you don't like to think about, Mitch?

chronologically through history, covering the Spanish-American War, invasion of the Philippines, World War I and II, the Civil Rights Movement, and the Vietnam War, while also covering lesser-known events such as the Pullman Strike, the Ludlow Massacre, and the Jitterbug Riot.

A People's History of American Empire challenges standard history lessons by presenting the perpetual cycle of violence, greed, and deceit too often propagated by those in power, showing the history of the United States that your history classes (at least, your pre-college classes) probably didn't tell you.[71]

---

71 And, for those of you who prefer your history with a few less pictures, there's Zinn's *A People's History of the United States*, which is the non-graphic precursor to this graphic novel.

Zinn recounts the banning of zoot suits after the Zoot Suit Riots in 1943.

PERSEPOLIS

Written by/art by: Marjane Satrapi • Published by: Pantheon; 2004

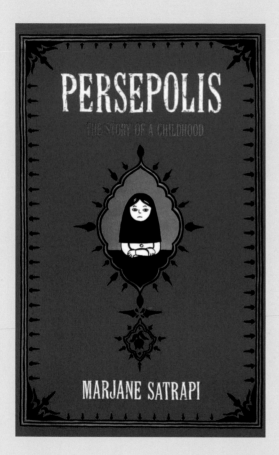

Marjane Satrapi's autobiographical tale of her childhood growing up in Iran depicts the atrocities of the Iranian conflicts of the 1980s through the eyes of a smart, but naïve, young girl struggling to understand the complexities of socio-cultural conflict.

Like many biographical works, *Persepolis* foregoes traditional story structure to build a narrative packed with hidden rooms and alcoves, each containing engrossing secrets of their own. She moves from moment to moment in her life, filling us in with vivacious depictions of people she's known—and the often sad endings to their lives. Satrapi's simple, clean art style effectively depicts darkness and tragedy without becoming overwhelmed with the gory details—what you see will sicken your soul, not your stomach.

As Marji grows older, she has to struggle with the rampant death and increasing loneliness which have become part of her day-to-day life. More and more of her loved ones are dead, gone, or left behind, until eventually even Marji herself is forced to leave Iran for safer grounds. It's only at the end of *Persepolis* that we see Marji beginning to really understand just how complicated things are—why she has to leave the only home she's ever known, why her parents can't leave, and why they're putting on a brave smile as they wave goodbye to her and die a little inside.

Greed often trumps ideology.

TO THE HEART OF THE STORM

Written by/art by: Will Eisner
Published by: Kitchen Sink Press, 1991; W.W. Norton & Company, 2008 (reprint edition)

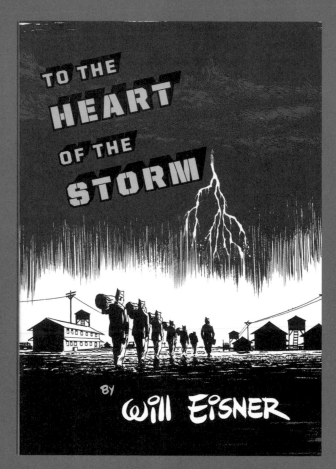

Eisner's autobiographical tale tells of his journey as an enlisted soldier heading into the heart of the storm itself—World War II—by recounting his upbringing and family history. It's hard not to read this and interpret Eisner as having a sour outlook on life. During childhood, he faced rampant discrimination due to his Jewish background, as did his mother, whose large family splintered under the stresses of city life, leaving her to care for her siblings as best she could (and her siblings to scatter in every direction, taking on adult responsibilities as children). Most men are generally depicted as greedy, serious-minded jerks, and most women as nagging shrews. Eisner often receives criticism for his depiction of non-white/non-male individuals in his stories, and *To the Heart of the Storm* only adds more fuel to such criticisms.

The early twentieth century was a hard time for most, with war and poverty ravaging the world, and Eisner pulls no punches in writing about it. Some modern autobiographies, with their focus on finding true loves and self-actualization, seem whiny and self-absorbed when compared with problems like violence, hunger, prejudice, and poverty. Eisner faces these tough topics head-on; the result is a story that is often unpleasant, but unflinching in its dedication to the truth.

Eisner's masterful use of body language make clear this man's frustrations.

BOXERS & SAINTS

Written by/art by: Gene Luen Yang • Published by: First Second; 2013

Most cultures believe in some sort of superstition: breaking a mirror brings seven years of bad luck, stepping on a crack breaks your mother's back, a dream about fish means someone will have a baby, and putting your hat on the bed will cause sickness. For China, and many other Asian countries, the number four is unlucky because its pronunciation sounds similar to "death."[72] Therefore, buildings won't label any floor with a four, giving four of anything is avoided, and April 4 is considered extremely bad luck. In *Saints*, when Vibiana is born on April 4 as the fourth daughter, she's immediately christened as the devil not even worthy of a name, leading her family to eventually call her Four-Girl.

Boxers and *Saints* are companion graphic novels by Gene Luen Yang, giving parallel accounts of the Boxer Rebellion from the vantage point of a person from each side. *Saints* showcases the Chinese-Christian perspective with Four-Girl (later given the Christian name Vibiana) whose abandonment from her family leaves her searching for a meaningful place in the world. Eventually she turns to Christianity, whose followers readily accept and value her, which places her on the side opposite of the Chinese rebels—the Boxers.

Boxers tells the point of view of the titular group, so named for their ritual of pre-battle pugilistic calisthenics believed to infuse themselves with the power of Gods. Bao, a boy from the same village as Vibiana, turns vengeful when Catholic missionaries harass, abuse, and disrespect his family, village, and religion. Bao then trains in martial arts and forms the Society of the Righteous and Harmonious Fists, a group of warriors hell-bent on eradicating Western influences from China—essentially, anyone identifying as Christian.

His quest leads him to Vibiana's Christian sanctuary, putting our two protagonists directly against each other.

Both *Boxers* and *Saints* compliment the other while standing on their own as complete, well-told adventures. Yang exhaustively researched the Boxer Rebellion to give authentic points of view to each side of the conflict. Not only does this create a

72 Similar to the way Americans often fear the number thirteen, or prudes fear the number sixty-nine.

fascinating dualism to each story, forcing you to think critically about who you're rooting for and who you're rooting against, it also illustrates the ways in which conflicting groups often both see themselves as noble and in the right while their enemies are vile and violent.[73]

Boxers isn't shy about drawing parallels between the Boxer rebels and extremist groups of today, chronicling the subtle transformation from freedom fighters to terrorists. At first, Bao and his group defend innocent civilians from the army sent to protect the Christians, but eventually they begin attacking innocent Christians unprovoked and ultimately make it their goal to wipe out all Christians. Yang went on to explain this comparison further, saying, "The Boxers have a lot in common with many of today's extremist movements in the Middle East. Little Bao would probably be labeled a terrorist if he were real and alive today. I tried to make him understandable, but not justified. The Boxers were defending a culture under attack. Yet—within my story, at least—their view of their own culture was incomplete." He then went on to add, "I also hope the books encourage readers to look at both sides of every conflict. The Internet age has brought about a blossoming of exaggerated righteous indignation. I've certainly been guilty of it. Maybe some of that will dissipate if we learn to look at both sides with compassion."[74]

The Society of the Righteous and Harmonious Fists perform rituals to be filled with the spirit of Gods before battle.

---

73 A faulty way of thinking known as the Mirror-Image Perception.

74 Quotes retrieved from: http://www.npr.org/2013/10/22/234824741/boxers-saints-compassion-quesions-for-gene-luen-yang.

CHAPTER 5

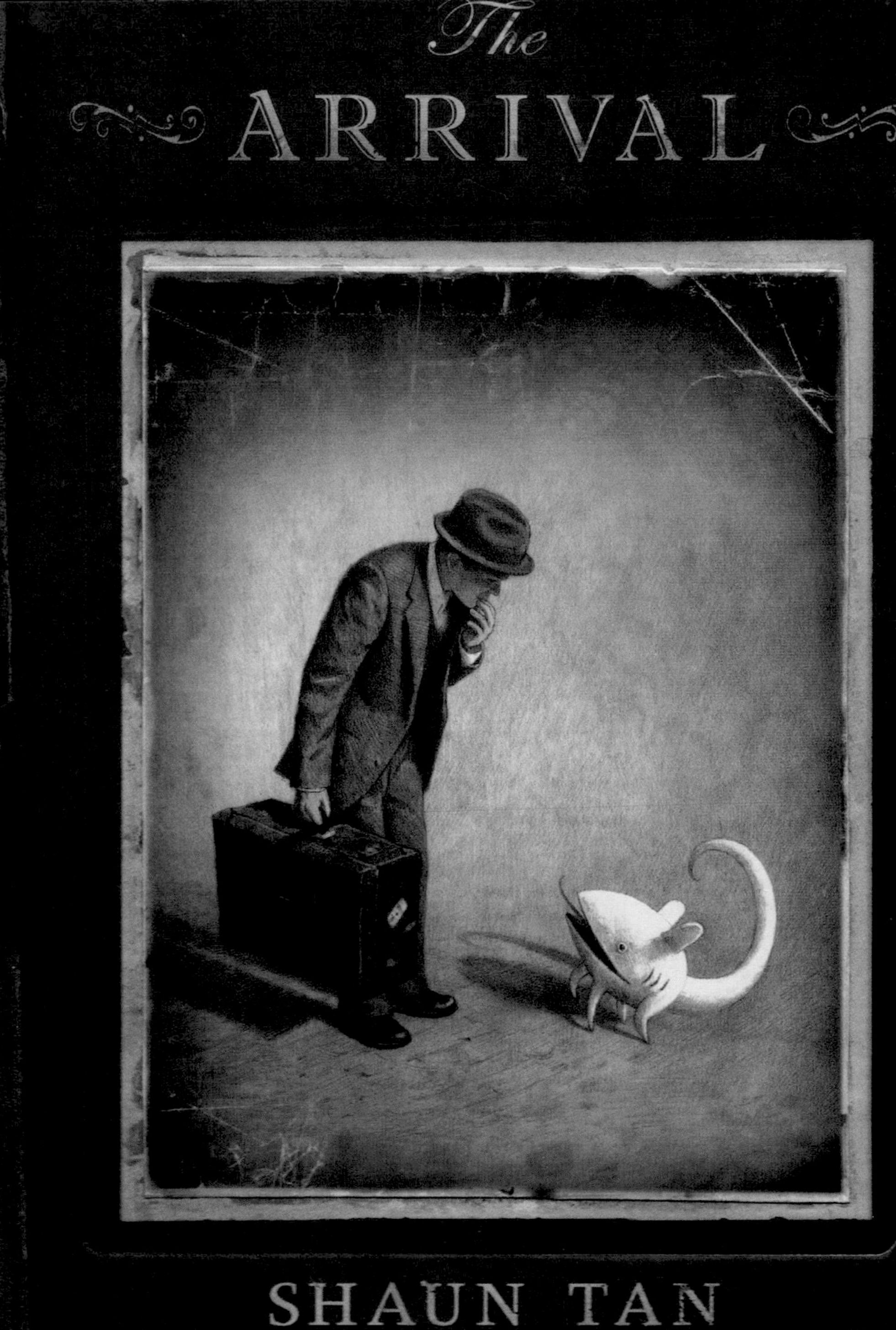
The
ARRIVAL
SHAUN TAN

FANTASY:
THE MENTAL HARD CANDY

///////////////////////

What makes a fantasy? Obviously there needs to be some sort of fantastic element to a story. If you're writing about two guys, a girl, and a pizza place, that's just a regular ol' drama or comedy. If your story is about two guys, a girl, a pizza place, and an amulet that summons the vicious phantasm of Gary Busey and the only way to cleanse this amulet is to complete the Seven Trials of Gary Busey, that, my friends, is a fantasy.

We like to think that fantasy stories are those supernatural tales with two primary elements. Firstly, they provide the reader with a piece of mental hard candy, that thing that their mind can savor all day and let them escape to some otherworldly place or situation. Secondly, while Science Fiction generally endeavors to (somewhat) base itself in reality in order to provide commentary on humanity, and Horror deals in the grisly and the macabre for insight, Fantasy provides commentary by ditching our reality and creating its own. *Star Wars*, for all its future tech and space aliens, is, at heart, a fantasy story—more than anything, it wants to take you to a galaxy far, far away.

The earliest fantasy stories are the fables and myths of ancient times. It was slow going at first, with only a handful of fantasy tales popping up over the course of hundreds of years. There are a few medieval-ish entries such as Shakespeare's *A Midsummer Night's Dream,* George MacDonald's *The Princess and the Goblin,* and *Sir Gawain and the Green Knight* by the Pearl Poet. Toward the twentieth century, fantasy became more common thanks to books like *The Wizard of Oz* series and *Alice in Wonderland.* Unfortunately, while these novels helped popularize the genre, they lead to people erroneously classifying fantasy as a children's genre. This decision wasn't changed for decades[75], even when J.R.R. Tolkien's *Lord of the Rings* trilogy arrived to revolutionize the scene. His seminal work created Middle-Earth, a fantastical realm full of goblins, dragons, treefolk, and little drunken people with hairy feet. It was an open, fertile field, inviting readers to come plant ideas and bask in what grew there. After the *Lord of the Rings,* however, the genre began to garner the respect it deserves and began getting classified as adult literature when appropriate.

In comics, *Weird Tales* told some of the earliest fantasy stories. Despite frequently dipping into the well of horror, *Weird Tales* also featured tales of

---

75 This misclassification as "children's stories" also plagued graphic novels. Back then if you wrote fantasy graphic novels, people must have assumed they were stories for babies still in the womb.

heroic daring in the face of magical opposition. *Kull* the conqueror, destroyer, and king brought sword-and-sandals action to comics alongside his more well-known barbarian brother, Conan. Both comics featured muscle-bound images of masculinity pummeling their way through countless foes during their rise to power. *Kull* tended to favor more … unusual threats than Conan—Lovecraftian things unknowable in their power or intent—and so he fostered a smaller, but devoted, fanbase.

The 1970s saw a massive boom in fantasy comics thanks in no small part to the success of Gary Gygax's *Dungeons and Dragons*[76]. Most of the fantasy comics of the '70s tended to be higher fantasy than their sword-and-sandal predecessors. Magic (and magical beings) were everywhere, and damn near every other farmhand was secretly the heir to the throne and a magical +5 sword of ass-kicking. These stories cut to the heart of what makes Fantasy such a wonderful genre—like Tolkien before them, they invited readers to join imaginative landscapes filled with fun and adventure.

More recently, Fantasy has expanded beyond the scope of medieval times, magic, and monsters. Neil Gaiman's *Sandman* blends contemporary sensibilities with dreamy fantasy and features Dream/Morpheus/The Sandman as its protagonist (along with a host of other anthropomorphized, conceptual characters such as Death, Desire, and Despair). *Fables* reimagines classic fairy-tale characters as living in modern times. *Excalibur* takes several X-Men favorites and puts them on dimension-hopping adventures each issue.

Many modern Fantasy stories rely on one primary fantastic element, such as *Seconds'* time travel or *Y: The Last Man*'s male-eradicating plague, which instantly eradicates (almost) every male creature on Earth. Like most genres, just what *is* Fantasy is, largely, up to the reader and author to decide. Regardless of how you define it, Fantasy as a genre of comics and graphic novels is one rich with imagination, eager for readers to plumb its pages and discover its many treasures.

---

76 There was even a pretty successful *Dungeons and Dragons* comic book series.

NIMONA

Written by/art by: Noelle Stevenson • Published by: HarperTeen; 2015

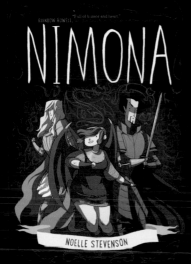

Lord Ballister Blackheart, the most fiendish villain in the kingdom, has teamed up with the shape-shifting Nimona to cause a reign of terror the likes of which the world has never seen! Only Ambrosius Goldenloin[77] can stop them (with the help of the Institution of Law Enforcement and Heroics, of course), and preserve peace across the land! Except that ... as it turns out, Lord Ballister Blackheart's not that bad, the Institute of Law Enforcement and Heroics isn't that heroic, and Nimona's ... complicated.

Noelle Stevenson flips conventions right and left with *Nimona*. Lord Ballister is a blend of *Buffy the Vampire Slayer*'s Giles, *Despicable Me*'s Gru, and Batman, using mad science and general mayhem to fight injustice in a medieval

77 Yes, those are their real names.

If you were a shapeshifter, why *wouldn't* you become a shark?

"AW, MAN, DO I HAVE TO DO THE BACKSTORY THING? IT'S KIND OF A DOWNER."
—NIMONA

Nimona ain't above shankin' fools.

GHOSTOPOLIS

Written by/art by: Doug TenNapel
Published by: GRAPHIX; 2010

No one knows for sure what happens to us when we die. If we're lucky, it'll be something like *Ghostopolis,* so we have an entire world full of spooky undead to hang out with as ghosts. Ghostopolis seems like a nice enough place to spend most of your afterlife. Or, it was a nice place, anyway. Lately it's been going downhill, and its spectral denizens are all too eager to sneak back to Earth and cause mischief. After slovenly ghost detective Frank Gallows (that's a detective who tracks down and apprehends ghosts, not a detective who is a ghost) accidentally sends the young (and alive) Garth Hale to Ghostopolis he enlists his ex girlfriend, ghost mechanic Claire Voyant (that's a mechanic who *is* a ghost, not a mechanic who repairs ghosts) to travel to this otherworld to get Garth back.

Despite the consistent air of death hanging over *Ghostopolis*, this is, by and large, a cheery adventure suitable for all ages. Doug TenNapel brews up a fun, imaginative ghost world full of mummies, zombies, will o' wisps, and (oddly)

world gone modern (there are shapeshifters and dragons, and also video calls and message boards. Go figure.) While such a combination would seem amateurishly random in the hands of a lesser writer, Stevenson makes this medieval, modern world work in hilarious fashion.

Nimona herself is a form-flipping flibbertigibbet who is easy to root for despite her tendency for killing guards and casual destruction. Stevenson's vivacious art keeps the energy flowing from panel to panel, and she knows exactly when to keep things moving along with a joke and when to let the characters breathe for a moment to reveal who they are.

> "NOW GHOSTOPOLIS IS A DUMP FULL OF CRIME AND BUGS. ALL GOOD GHOSTS DREAM OF ESCAPING TO EARTH."
> —CECIL HALE, GHOST GRAMPA

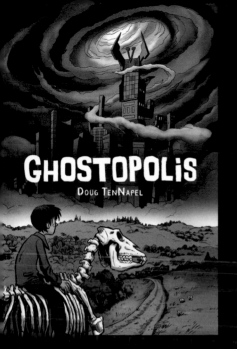

oblins; the world of Ghostopolis is am- packed with magic and secrets, nd the colorful art makes it easy o want to get lost in it. TenNapel as a long history of creating vild characters in works such as *Earthworm Jim*, *Skullmonkeys*, and *The Neverhood*; *Ghostopolis* keeps p the trend by being as overstuffed vith wonderful weirdos as your aunt's loset is stuffed with tacky sweaters. It ightly touches on themes of accepting eath and the past, but primarily, this a book about having fun

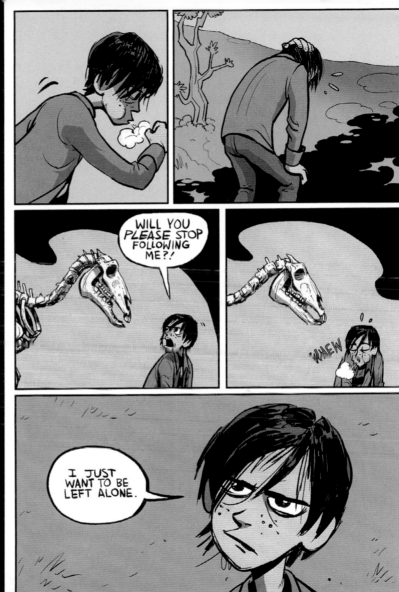

Garth Hale ain't in the mood for skeleton horse shenanigans.

SECONDS

Written by: Bryan Lee O'Malley • Art by: Bryan Lee O'Malley and Nathan Fischer • Published by: Ballantine Books; 2014

How do you follow up your life's work? How can you be sure that your decisions are the *right* decisions? With *Seconds,* both protagonist Katie and author/ artist Bryan Lee O'Malley seem to be asking these questions, and the answer is obvious: by abusing the hell out of magic mushrooms that let you time travel.

Master chef Katie Clay crushed it with her first job at a major restaurant, Seconds, by cooking smart, kickass food everyone seems to like. Now she's ready to strike out on her own and open a restaurant that actually *belongs* to her instead of just being head chef at an awesome eatery. But opening a restaurant is hard, and there's about a zillion decisions to be made, and between her rocky new business opportunity and even rockier love life, Katie's trapped in an eternal web of self-doubt. Hell, she even second-guesses *Seconds'* narrator and argues with her constantly. While dealing with this existential crisis, Katie meets Lis, a house spirit with a fabulous fashion sense. Lis gives her access to a

one-time ticket to time travel-ville, letting her undo any single decision she's ever regretted. Of course, like any fan of fine food, Katie can't resist going back for more and continues abusing time travel until chronology is so screwed-up that even the Doctors Brown and Who would throw their hands up in the air and call it a day.

As evidenced by the *Scott Pilgrim* series, O'Malley has a knack for creating animated characters whose dialogue flows off the page with a lyrical humor. His art enhances the humor and his unique syntagmatic choices bring style and vigor to every panel, whether it's a birds-eye-view of the chaos of a restaurant, a high-energy onomatopoeia smashing someone in the face, or history itself unraveling. Still, there are moments of quiet dread which O'Malley delivers through in-depth analyses of spaces; we all have a space we consider our own, and O'Malley shows how those spaces, no matter how isolated, connect and affect each other. As these spaces are compromised, so, too, are the characters' sense of safety and identity.

Seconds style still bears some of the manga-esque elements found in *Scott Pilgrim* while evolving in a different direction to include more European influences, particularly through the huge, sweeping background spaces found throughout the novel. O'Malley drew from numerous influences in creating such landscapes, citing Kerascoët's *Beauté* as "an obsession," continuing on to say, "I certainly made a conscious effort to go more Euro, less manga in this one, just to suit the vibe of the story."[78]

While, broadly speaking, *Seconds* muses on the difficulties of understanding that our actions have long-reaching consequences we can't always predict, it also seems to be a personal meditation by O'Malley on his career. The *Scott Pilgrim* series was an unprecedented success, selling millions of copies and even getting a cult-hit theatrical film adaptation, likely leaving O'Malley satisfied with his past work while feeling paralyzed with the fear that his next work wouldn't be as well-received. Fortunately, both he and *Seconds'* protagonist Katie manage to push through that fear. In O'Malley's case, he created *Seconds,* a terrific follow-up to what was his most famous work at the time, and in Katie's case, she learns that regret is just a part of life. We each make thousands of decisions every day. We *hope* they'll all work out, but we also know they won't, so all we can do is keep moving forward and not become too obsessed with our pasts.

78 Retrieved from: www.slate.com/articles/arts/ books/2014/07/interview_with_scott_pilgrim_writer_ bryan_lee_o_malley_about_his_new_graphic.html.

O'Malley ignores conventions to employ emotive descriptions like the one floating above Hazel's head.

CASTLE WAITING

Written by/art by: Linda Medley • Published by: Fantagraphics; 2006

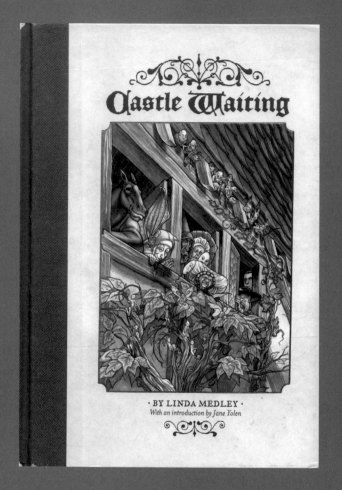

Fantasy worlds are often ugly places, full of vicious monsters, brutal rulers, and sexually aggressive bandits—it's often kill or be killed. As the pregnant and wayward Jain discovers, the world of *Castle Waiting* is a land entirely unlike the others. Here the people are (mostly) gentle, the adventures cheerful, and pretty much everyone knows how to play nice.

With *Castle Waiting*, Linda Medley creates a medley of her own, mixing new characters and situations with classic fairy tales and myths. After Sleeping Beauty awoke, she ran off to immediately get hitched, leaving her newly uncursed waiting staff with little to do but manage the castle grounds and wait around. When the pregnant Jain arrives, the staff is overjoyed at having this new visitor and the bounding bundle of joy she's soon to bring, and gleefully take her in. The motley cast of bearded nuns, handsome horsemen, and stickly storks swap stories with Jain, telling of their past adventures in great detail. In the traditional sense, little happens in *Castle Waiting*; there's no larger story, nor any great evil brewing to dislodge the castle's happy residents. But through these seemingly-unrelated stories, Medley crafts an emotional throughline of the importance of supporting one another, and how it's not greed, nor strength, but kindness, which is the greatest "power" of all.

Jain finally arrives at Castle Waiting.

DAYTRIPPER

Written by/art by: Fábio Moon and Gabriel Bá • Published by: Vertigo; 2011

Bras de Olivias Dominguez writes obituaries. Good ones. He's also dying. Or dead. Or alive. In the lofty, confusing, and trippy *Daytripper*, Moon and Bá explore Bras and his various moments of potential deadness while musing on family, being alive, and the things we place importance on.

Daytripper leaps from moment to moment in Bras' life with aplomb, showing us the most important stuff with a casual, yet thoughtful, style. Throughout Bras' life we see the way his decisions affect him and those around him; no matter how isolated we try to be, our lives are inextricably interconnected. Death looms over every chapter (especially since Bras dies at the end of each one). While, at first, these deaths are tragic, as *Daytripper* progresses, the tragedy gives way to understanding.

"No book is complete without its end. And once you get there ... only when you read the last words will you see how good the book is." -Bras

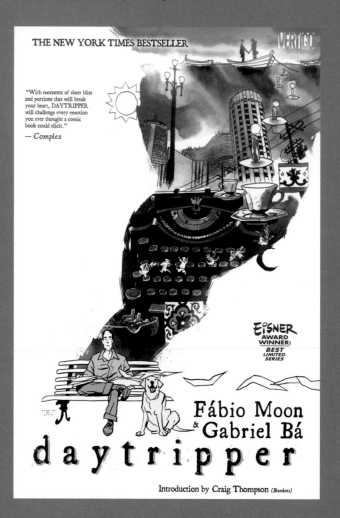

Their eyes meet across
a crowded room.

Y: THE LAST MAN

Written by: Brian K. Vaughan • Art by: Pia Guerra • Published by: Vertigo; beginning in 2002

What would the world be like without men in it? That's the question posed by *Y: The Last Man*. Things would be chaotic for a while (as they would be after any event affecting a huge portion of the human population), and those who are still left would see a serious shift in social dynamics. Brian K. Vaughan explores gender dynamics in this post-apocalyptic tale of the last known man in a world full of women.

Vaughan's famous for his sharp-tongued writing, and *Y: The Last Man* is a clear example of why. Despite the frequently shifting time frame and locale of the narrative, *Y: The Last Man* stays easy to follow thanks to memorable characters and a strong pacing. Yorick, as the last living male on Earth, is something of a commodity, and so with the help of some people much more competent and intelligent than he, he goes on a road trip to find the right science-y person to try to science up a cure for this male-destroying plague.

As you might expect, the concept of gender inequality comes up quite a bit, with some women in despair over the loss of the men, some overjoyed, and others indifferent. Though it's generally handled pretty deftly, there are

WINNER OF THREE EISNER AWARDS

"The best graphic novel I've ever read."
—STEPHEN KING

Y

THE LAST MAN

BOOK ONE

BRIAN K. VAUGHAN

PIA GUERRA

JOSÉ MARZÁN, JR.

VERTIGO

"IN THE SUMMER OF 2002, A PLAGUE OF UNKNOWN ORIGIN DESTROYED EVERY LAST SPERM, FETUS, AND FULLY DEVELOPED MAMMAL WITH A Y CHROMOSOME— WITH THE APPARENT EXCEPTION OF ONE YOUNG MAN AND HIS PET, A MALE CAPUCHIN MONKEY." –NARRATION

moments where the lack of a female writer/co-writer is felt, such as a moment when one character references the myth of "menstrual synch-up" leading to an entire town being on edge during that time of the month, a myth that has long been debunked. Had a woman written/co-written this story, this myth may not have been included as fact.

Regardless, outside of a few minor quibbles, *Y: The Last Man* paints an engrossing tale of a world without men, balancing post-apocalyptic themes with real-world gender commentary and character-driven humor.

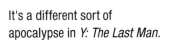

It's a different sort of apocalypse in *Y: The Last Man.*

ZITA THE SPACEGIRL

Written by/art by: Ben Hatke • Published by: First Second; 2011

Author Anais Nin once said, "Each friend represents a world in us, a world possibly not born until they arrive, and it is only by this meeting that a new world is born."[79]

Zita the Spacegirl takes Anais Nin's words to heart to show us the figurative (and literal) ways friends show us new worlds.

A meteoroid crashes to the Earth. Embedded in it is a remote with a big, red button. It's a well-known rule that, when you see a big red button, you push that big red button to see what happens. Zita and her friend, Joseph, obey this rule out of curiosity, leading to the creation of a portal to an alien world. From this portal emerges gnarly tentacles that grab Joseph and yank him in. Zita, being the good friend that she is, leaps in after him.

Zita the Spacegirl contains plenty of standard story tropes—doomsday countdowns, imperiled kidnapees, long journeys—but it's the pervasive message of friendship, of putting others before yourself, which elevates *Zita* above the rest. On her journey to save Joseph, despite the end of the world looming over this alien new world, Zita takes the time to talk to and help out every creature she meets, resulting in the birth of countless new friendships.

Ben Hatke excels at creating adorable creatures whose personality shines through their character designs. Despite Zita's new friends being otherworldly and mechanical, Hatke still imbues them with endearingly human elements; after reading *Zita the Spacegirl,* you'll want to go on your own quest to befriend every robot, beast, and space weirdo you meet.

79 Retrieved from: https://en.wikiquote.org/wiki/Ana%C3%AFs_Nin.

Zita's got no respect for the classics.

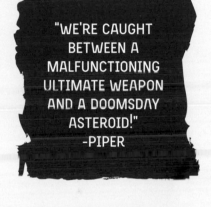

THE UNDERWATER WELDER

Written by/art by: Jeff Lemire • Published by: Top Shelf Productions; 2012

Many of us keep the past close to our hearts. Whether it's for nostalgic reasons or regretful ones, it's hard to let go of what's happened, and Jeff Lemire captures these difficulties with the precision of a marksman in *The Underwater Welder,* a metaphor-laden ghost story about kids idealizing a parent, desperately trying to have a relationship with an absent parent, and getting stuck in the past.

Lemire's protagonist, Jack, is an imperfect man with problems, faults, and fears. An everyman. Jack's father died on a diving excursion when he was a young boy. Guilt and the lack of closure from his father's body never being found creates an obsession in Jack, who chases his father's ghost by adopting the same obsession that cost him his life. By becoming an underwater welder, Jack tries to feel closer to his father while gaining an easy excuse to pull away from his pregnant wife and his fears of parenthood. During one of his dives, a mysterious happening gives Jack the thing he's always wanted, transporting

"I WASTED SO MUCH TIME LOOKING BACK THAT I HAVEN'T LET MYSELF LOOK FORWARD." –JACK

Time travel does a number on a person's brain.

him to a deserted town where he can relive the past he yearns for so much.

The Underwater Welder encourages readers to live in the moment, to love the people in front of you instead of forever chasing someone you can't reach. As Barry "The Flash" Allen says, "Life is locomotion. If you're not moving, you're not living."[80]

80 *The Flash*, Volume 4, #1, Berganza, Buccalato, & Manapul.

Written by/art by: Mark Siegel • Published by: First Second; 2012

Mermaids aren't always of the cheerful, redheaded, singing variety. In many stories, mermaids lead unwary sailors to their doom, enticing them with their beautiful appearances and golden voices. In *Sailor Twain*, one such seaman finds himself in a similar situation, tempted into obsession by his new mermaid "friend," South.

Sailor Twain, accomplished young riverboat captain, happens to stumble upon a mortally wounded mermaid. Being the stalwart man he is, Twain rescues the mermaid and begins nursing her back to health in secret, finding that his writing grows more inspired with every second he spends in her company and further from his duties as captain, husband, and person. Meanwhile, the riverboat's owner, LaFayette, desperately hunts for something ... but Twain's not sure what. Could it be that LaFayette, too, knows the touch of a mermaid? Is he trying to find his way back to his own aquatic beauty? Perhaps steal Twain's new "friend" away from him? Or is there something else going on ... some darker reason as to why South is prone to bouts of detachment, or some explanation as to her cruel sense of humor and her odd desire to entice Twain to abandon his life on land?

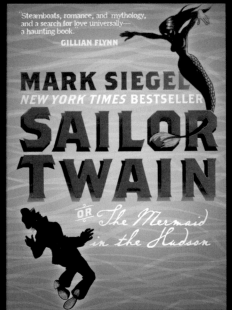

Much like the mermaid South herself, *Sailor Twain* enchants readers from the first moment they lay eyes on it. Siegel's gorgeous graphite art gives life to his characters and a constant sense of wetness to the river and its surroundings.

Siegel's work is fantastically well-researched, dripping with details specific to the era and location and occasionally making use of 1800s American-style lettering, background art, and scene transitions to further set the sense of time. Those well-versed in Western literature will likely delight in the frequent, often subtle, allusions Siegel makes to masters of prose such as Virginia Wolfe, Emily Dickinson, and, of course, Mark Twain.

In much the same way Junji Ito had to become obsessed with spirals to pen *Uzumaki*, so, too, would it seem, that Siegel became obsessed with researching literature and riverboat culture circa 1800s America to create *Sailor Twain*. The result is a haunting, melancholic, magical tale with a distinct sense of romance, mythology, and realism.

Siegel employs simple, often geometric, shapes where he can to provide his characters with greater iconography.

THE PRINCESS AND THE PONY

Written by/art by: Kate Beaton • Published by: Arthur A. Levine Books; 2015

Pinecone, a warrior princess, has a birthday coming up, and she not-so-subtly spells out that she wants her parents to get her a big horse she can ride into battle. Why? Because that's what warriors do—they fight things. When her parents get a small, fat, not-so-perfect pony, Pinecone becomes very disappointed. Whatever will she do with such a useless steed? A steed with a farting problem, no less.

Kate Beaton manages to create an adorable story with an admirable life lesson using fewer words than are in this review. *The Princess and the Pony* shows us that you shouldn't disregard something just because it isn't exactly what you wanted. The warrior princess Pinecone decides to give her little pony a chance, and ends up learning that there are different sides to people (and battle) that she never thought about before. Beaton also reverses the idea of being a "strong woman." It doesn't always mean physically kicking ass to make a difference in the world. Rather, being a strong woman can be kicking ass through the spread of new ideas, or standing against the majority when it would be easier to quietly go along with the group. Also that, sometimes, it's okay for a tough warrior to trade in the armor for a cute, cozy sweater.

Beaton is a master of expression, bringing huge characters to life with the stroke of a few lines, and The Princess and the Pony's colorful art and diverse characters give an unstoppable sense of fun to every page.

Parents looking for a book to read to their child

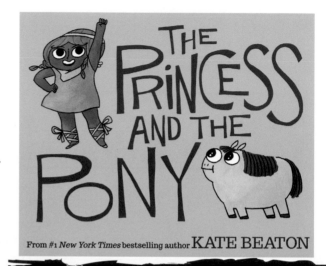

"THE LITTLE PONY WAS SO EXCITED, IT LIFTED ITS TAIL AND FARTED." —NARRATOR, WHO ISN'T NECESSARILY BRITISH BUT IT SEEMS FITTING TO IMAGINE THAT WAY

that doesn't make them want to poke their eyes out from having to read it a thousand times, look no further than *The Princess and the Pony*. Never have we ever so instantly fallen in love with a book as we did with this one. It may technically be a children's book, but it's still kind of a graphic novel and we love it and Kate Beaton, so it's going in this book, goshdangit.[81]

---

81 It should probably come with a couple of warnings, though, such as "Warning: You may suffer from cuteness overload after reading," and "Warning: You may develop a cozy sweater addiction from this book."

Princess Pinecone got a lot of cozy sweaters.
Warriors do not need cozy sweaters.

Being a warrior princess, Pinecone thinks she doesn't need any cozy sweaters, or a silly, fat pony.

BEHIND THE INK: KATE BEATON

While Kate Beaton's foray into the field of graphic novels is a relatively new thing, her contributions to the medium of comics and webcomics are both long-running and immense. Beaton's *Hark! A Vagrant* series points out the comedy in history, often by turning a spotlight on true historical facts. Jules Verne sends Edgar Allan Poe fanboy letters telling him they should be friends and also that he should feature more balloons in his stories. America's founding fathers find themselves transported in time into modern-day malls and amusement parks, stunned and bewildered by what they find there (except for Benjamin Franklin, who loves that stuff because he was a chillaxin' genius).

Some comics feature decidedly un-famous historical figures to poke fun at the weird norms of the time, like girls giving handkerchiefs to their paramours (handkerchiefs no doubt infused with boogs), or the two medieval peasants in love who frolic in the fields while one comments to the other, "I've like, never ever brushed my teeth,"[82] or the silliness of the entire Irish-American invasion of Canada.

Beaton's brilliance is in her ability to come at a subject from a novel angle, giving life and humor to people and moments often described with textbook dryness. Beaton manages to find the funny in the most odd of occurrences, pleasing and educating audiences at the same time.

PROMINENT WORKS:
• *The Princess and the Pony* (2015)
• *Step Aside, Pops* (2015)
• *Hark! A Vagrant* (2011)
• *Never Learn Anything from History* (2009)

THE ARRIVAL

Written by/art by: Shaun Tan • Published by: Arthur A. Levine Books; 2007

Our hero has arrived.

To leave one's own country to make a home in another takes bravery and determination. In *The Arrival,* Shaun Tan tells the story of immigrants arriving in a foreign land with the hope of creating a better life for themselves and their families.

A family of three—father, mother, and daughter—live in a land darkened by monstrous, looming shadows growing darker by the day. The father immigrates to a new country hoping to find a safe home for his family, wrestling with the new cultures, language, and rituals he finds there while getting to know other immigrant neighbors. Tan wordlessly conveys confusion of immigrants in a new country through the use of alien symbols, technology, creatures, and architecture. Everything in this new country is foreign to readers and protagonist alike; his struggle to gain understanding is *our* struggle.

Tan conducted lengthy research to prepare for *The Arrival,* taking countless reference photos and examining archived images and accounts of immigrants arriving to locations like Ellis Island. The rich, sepia-tone of the artwork and

photorealism of the people juxtaposed with the otherworldliness of its non-human elements create a story that feels inarguably true to the immigrant experience, and Tan's decision to eschew dialogue makes this experience universally understandable. Inscrutable symbols litter the world; like a foreigner struggling to speak the language, readers will automatically try to infer meaning to the various signs and warnings all around.

Even if the story had somehow ended up being utter dreck, *The Arrival* is an absolute feast for the eyes. You'll want to savor every detail on the page, whether it's the amazing, geometrically-inspired cityscape, the emotionally-evocative images of war and longing, or the little details in a puff of smoke or an adorable creature. Shaun Tan's *The Arrival* is second-to-none; not only is it one of the finest graphic novels ever put to print, it's one of the finest stories ever published.

Through Tan's rich art, readers can understand much, even without dialogue.

CHAPTER 6

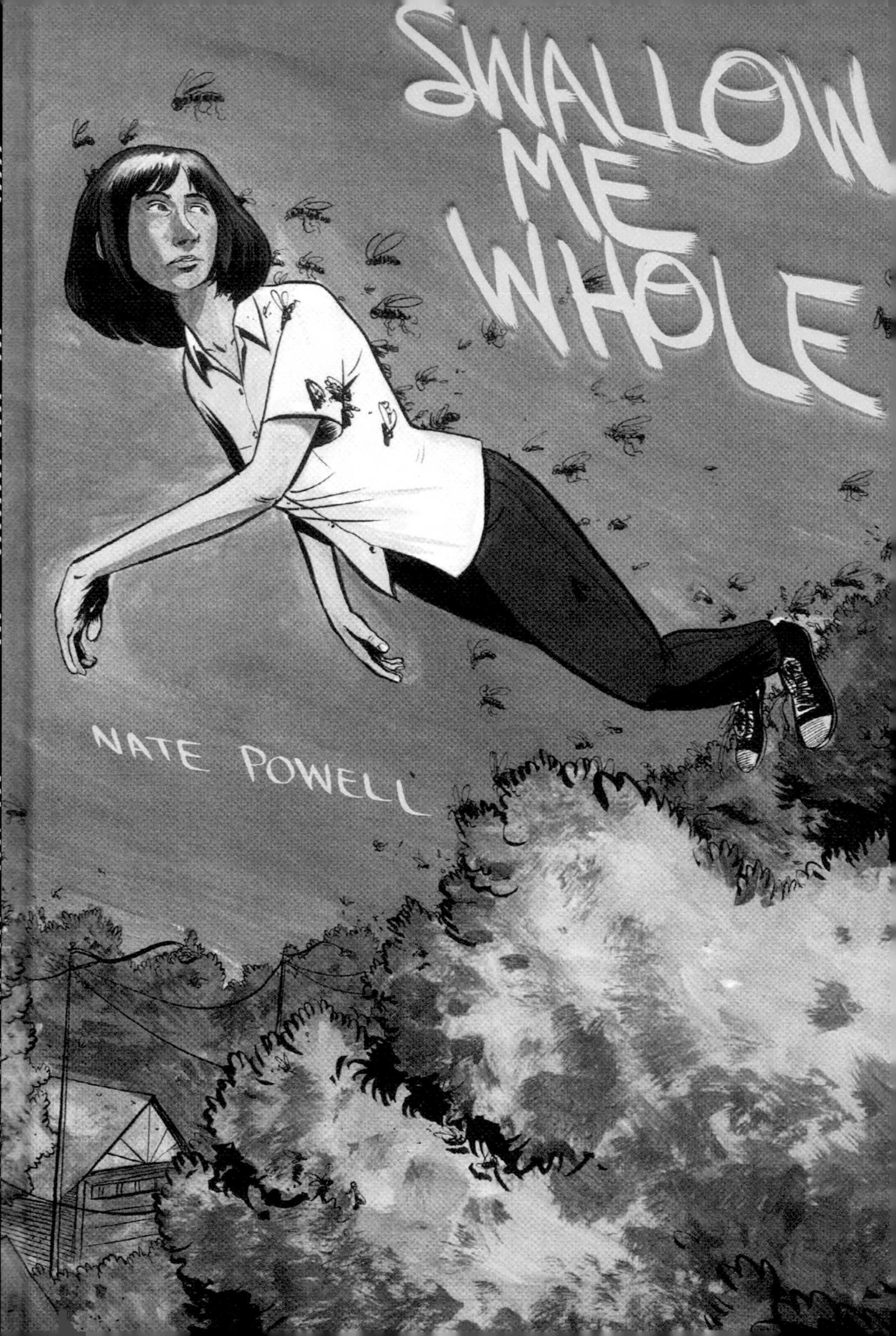
SWALLOW
ME
WHOLE
NATE POWELL

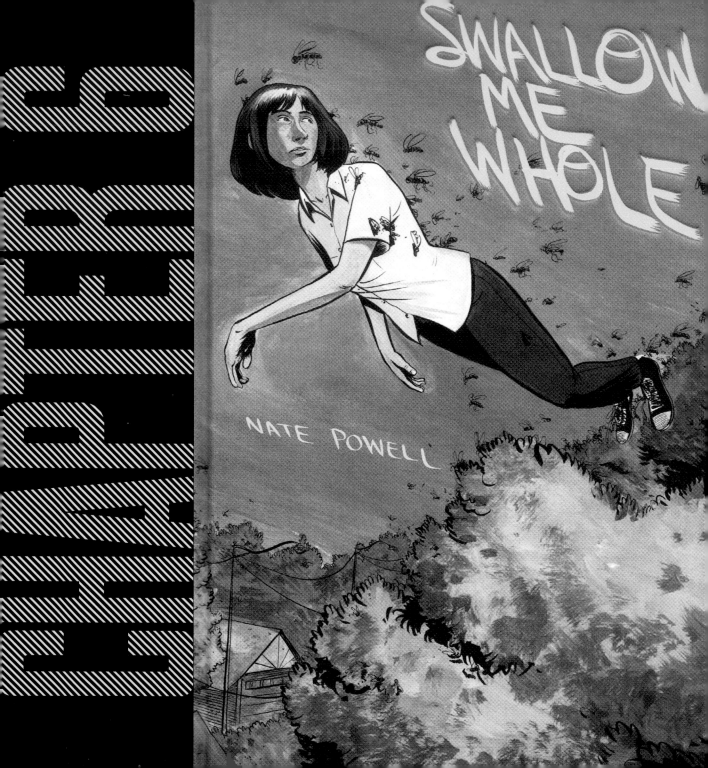

MODERN DRAMA: THE HERE AND NOW OF NOW AND THEN

/////////////////////////

For modern dramas, the era in which they're set is like a koala's opinion on space exploration—it doesn't really matter. You could have a story set in 1995, but if that's not the lynchpin of your tale, it's probably a modern drama. Speculative fiction like science fiction, fantasy, or horror use unreal elements to highlight real issues. Historical literature examines the past to better understand the present. Modern dramas, on the other hand, tend to be more intimate, smaller in scope, more about a handful of individuals rather than larger social movements. They're focused on the present (or the so-recent-it's-basically-present) instead of the distant past

Some of the earliest examples of "modern" dramas in American comics comes from newspaper strips such as *Mary Worth* and *Apartment 3-G*. Started in 1938, *Mary Worth* featured the titular character, an older woman living in New York City, dispensing matronly advice to the people around her as they tackled issues such as love, addiction, and the stressors of everyday life. Decades later, *Apartment 3-G* followed *Mary Worth*'s example, though its drama tended to be a bit more romantic and soap opera-esque in its presentation. Both comics rarely veer into high-stakes storytelling, but their gentle comic strip realism present a shifting presentation of the struggles of the modern era (whenever that happened be).

As newspaper comics fall away with the inevitable death of the newspaper,[83] fans of modern dramas turn to webcomics and graphic novels to get their fill. Webcomics such as *Questionable Content*, or *Menage a 3* each have their own take on drama, with the former's propensity for indie rock humor and mild sci-fi elements, and the latter's tendency for sexy comedy, but they both give (semi)realistic takes on the human problems of life and love, generally staying focused on small groups of characters.

Unlike newspaper strips and webcomics, which rely on keeping readers relatively uplifted and entertained on a frequent basis, graphic novels can afford to get much darker and more reflective. *Stitches,* for example, often takes entire pages or multiple pages to depict short sequences of the character running or reacting to something. *Unlikely* often ends pages and sequences without any semblance of a comedic or philosophical punchline, instead building toward a particular sentiment from start to finish. Graphic novels have the luxury of being able to take their time crafting a story which builds on itself as a whole rather than having to add to a story, piece-by-piece, the way webcomics do.

---

83 "Print is dead." —Egon Spengler, *Ghostbusters*.

An Exploration of Self

Cartoonists have a higher-than-average tendency to use graphic novels as an autobiographical exploration, using artistic style to better express the true feelings of their life rather than the literal truth of each moment. Comics autobiographies are sometimes melancholy examinations of troubled pasts, thoughtful contemplations of their quests for self-actualizations, or personal accounts of troubled moments in history.[84]

Justin Brown's *Binky Brown Meets the Holy Virgin Mary* is considered by many to be the first autobiographical graphic novel; it tells the struggles Brown went through as a young man battling his Obsessive-Compulsive Disorder while living under his parents strict Catholic rule. Harvey Pekar (*American Splendor)* spent years telling disjointed, autobiographical tales in an attempt to broaden the medium of comics. Pekar stated:

"When I was a little kid, and I was reading these comics in the '40s, I kind of got sick of them because after a while, they were just formulaic. I figured there was some kind of a flaw that keeps them from getting better than they are, and then when I saw Robert Crumb's work in the early '60s, when he moved from Philadelphia to Cleveland, and he moved around the corner from me, I thought 'Man, comics are where it's at'."[85]

Autobiographical comics, being more up-close in nature, often cover topics which are avoided or considered taboo by mainstream pop culture.

Binky Brown Meets the Holy Virgin Mary, Marbles, and *Voyeurs* all give firsthand accounts of dealing with mental illness. *Blankets* and *Fun Home* detail the awkward early years of sexual exploration. *The Story of My Tits* and *Epileptic* cover cancer and, as you might expect, epilepsy. Despite how commonly we have encountered mental illness, or the ways in which we all explore our sexualities, these topics are still discussed furtively; autobiographical comics draw their roots from underground comix, a genre which proudly flies its middle finger in the face of societal norms, and through this boldly oppositional perspective we find a greater truth.

---

84 The latter of which would be found in the Historical Literature chapter, not here, silly.

85 Heater, Brian. *A Book Called Malice.*

MARBLES

Written by/art by: Ellen Forney • Published by: Avery; 2012

Bipolar disorder: a broad term for a group of disorders primarily characterized by alternating states of *mania,* a wildly optimistic, energized, reckless, and shortsighted state, and *depression,* a chronic state of feeling sadness, joyless, worthless, and without energy. Bipolar disorder affects nearly six million Americans, with a number of famous creative types suffering from the disorder. In *Marbles,* creative type Ellen Forney gives a stark account of coming to terms with her own bipolar disorder and the ensuing struggle to find the thing she never thought she wanted: balance.

Free-spirited. Imaginative. Talkative. Bold. Ellen had always described herself as these things, never putting too much thought into what these qualities might actually mean, nor thinking about the bouts of blueness she frequently slipped into. After a psychiatrist opens her eyes to the fact that these qualities are indicative of bipolar disorder, Ellen struggles to get this wildly vacillating disorder under control. She works with her psychiatrist to find the right combination of therapy, cognitive/behavior training, and medication, to keep her highs from getting so high and her lows from getting so low. Sure, those manic phases seem great—who

wouldn't want to feel boundlessly optimistic, energized, and creative? But with them comes the problem of recklessness—overcommitting your time, not thinking about the consequences of your action, that sort of thing—and those manic states are the top of the rollercoaster gathering momentum for when they drop off into the inevitable depression. Forney recounts the highs and lows with vivid detail; as a cartoonist, she's always sketching, and *Marbles* includes a number of sketches from both manic and depressed episodes alike, stark, haunting, *tortured* images of when she was trying to lift herself out of a fog of misery and reel herself back from the revved-up edge.

Forney also explores the duality between creativity and inner turmoil, examining the numerous creative types who suffered from mental illnesses, particularly bipolar disorder. Vincent Van Gogh, Sylvia Plath, Tennessee Williams, Mark Twain, Leo Tolstoy ... the list goes on and on.

Forney recalls her fears that her creativity and mental disorder were inextricably linked; should she finally find that state of balance, her ability to think creatively might vanish. For all its heavy themes of suicide and mental health, *Marbles* is a surprisingly fun read. Forney has a knack for articulating her

READING WAS AN EFFORT, THOUGH. I BOUGHT SOME OF MY FAVORITE CHILDHOOD BOOKS AT A USED BOOKSTORE — THE TYPE WAS BIGGER, THE LANGUAGE LESS DEMANDING, & THE STORIES PREDICTIBLY SAFE.

I READ THEM SLOWLY, GAZING LENGTHILY AT THE ILLUSTRATIONS.

Newberry Award Winning Classic
A WRINKLE IN TIME
Madeleine L'Engle

THE PHANTOM TOLLBOOTH
NORTON JUSTER
Illos by JULES FEIFFER

Mary Poppins
P.L. TRAVERS

I GOT COMPLETELY LOST IN THEM.

The Lion, the Witch, and the Wardrobe
C.S. LEWIS
The Chronicles of Narnia

WHEN I'D FINISH THE LAST PAGE, I'D BE HALF-SURPRISED AND SO DISAPPOINTED TO FIND MYSELF BACK IN THE JOYLESS REALITY OF MY APARTMENT.

Ellen Forney recalls the joy and dismay of reading while depressed.

thoughts with quick energy and intelligence, and her art enhances the mood of each page. While recalling manic phases of her life, Forney uses ornamented, multidirectional, lively art to illustrate those feelings of mania. When depression sets in, the ornamentation and excess linework vanish—instead the art becomes small, undetailed. A struggle to get on the page. Forney's shifting styles do a phenomenal job of illustrating this tumultuous condition.

Though the battle to achieve balance is both emotional and financially draining, it's one well-worth going on. Bipolar disorder is a difficult condition to live with, both for the person who has it and the people around them; Forney's brave account of her determined personal journey shows that balance *can* be found, that it's good to forgo the heavensward highs of mania and the obliterating lows of depression to, instead, achieve a state of equilibrium and peace.

Written by/art by: Alison Bechdel • Published by: Houghton Mifflin, 2006; Mariner Books, 2007

"A splendid autobiography . . . refreshingly open and generous."
— *Entertainment Weekly*

Fun Home

A FAMILY TRAGICOMIC

ALISON BECHDEL

MARINER BOOKS

"IN OUR PARTICULAR REENACTMENT OF THIS MYTHIC RELATIONSHIP, IT WAS NOT ME BUT MY FATHER WHO WAS TO PLUMMET FROM THE SKY."
—ALISON BECHDEL

When you hear "fun home," you might think it's about a house that's ... well, *fun*. Maybe a graphic novel equivalent to that classic family sitcom *Full House,* complete with precocious kids and annoying catch phrases. In the case of Alison Bechdel's *Fun Home,* the name refers to her family's business: a *funeral* home. Saying a funeral home is fun might seem like a tenuous argument, but somehow Bechdel, who grew up playing/ working in the mortuary, manages to put the fun in funeral. Sometimes. Sometimes it's just miserable there, of course, like any family workplace where you're dealing with dead bodies all the time and your dad is as cold as the corpses.

This autobiographical work from Bechdel shares her uncanny childhood with unabashed honesty. Her father, Bruce, appeared to be the ideal husband and father. Bruce was also emotionally-neglectful and a closeted homosexual who stepped into the path of a moving vehicle (Bechdel describes the act as deliberate), leaving her without support or guidance.

Bruce was enthusiastic about literature, heavily influencing Alison's passion for reading; as a result, *Fun Home* is riddled with references from classics like *Ulysses, The Odyssey,* and *Colette.* Bechdel ardently draws parallels to literature to extract understanding from her life events.

The format is labyrinthine; events are covered and re-covered as the audience gains new insight into what's happening. Bechdel fondly looks back at some of the good times in her life while still being investigative and critical of her relationship with her father. Bechdel

Note the joyless expressions and uncomfortable body language here.

also covers other important, yet often undiscussed, subjects such as homosexuality, masturbation, emotionally unavailable parents, and suicide. Bechdel draws her characters with detached facial expressions and frigid body language to create an atmosphere of emotional distance.

Throughout *Fun Home,* Bechdel discusses what it was like living with parents willing to abdicate the emotional well-being of their children and discusses her struggles with the thought that one of her rare moments of attempted emotional connection—the letter through which she announced herself as being gay—precipitated her father's death.

Fun Home is packed with Bechdel's sophisticated, honest, hyper-verbose style of writing; it's an intellectual and honest cup of fresh coffee amidst a sea of stale sludge. Bechdel's penchant for esoteric words and references means that even the most well-read and verbose amongst us may need to turn to a reference guide on occasion, which is a good thing. The fact that Bechdel is helping you expand your vocabulary through the use of an emotionally-complex, provocative

IT'S A GOOD LIFE, IF YOU DON'T WEAKEN

Written by/art by: Seth • Published by: Drawn and Quarterly; 2003

Following in the treads of other introspective, underground comics artists such as Harvey Pekar and Robert Crumb, mononomial cartoonist Seth created *It's a Good Life, If You Don't Weaken,* a semi-autobiographical, self-reflective look at the neurotic artist's quest to understand his artistic ancestors.

Seth is obsessed with *The New Yorker*'s comics, particularly the comics of old, double-particularly the comics of one man known as Kalo.[86] Kalo only contributed a handful of comics to the newspaper, but Seth found the work so captivating, he launches himself on a casual, yet consuming, investigation. Seth is pretentious, and often up his own ass about his work, while having enough self-awareness to realize it. Seth dislikes the modern time he lives in, longing for the simpler times of the past—or, he admits, the idealized version of the simple past he envisions.

Much of *It's a Good Life* depicts the sort of homosocial maleness found in early twentieth century comics work; Seth's only friend is male, as is the subject of his obsession and most conversations revolve around the creations of male comics creators. Very few women were able to take part in early comics history, and fewer were depicted on the page as anything other than subordinates or objects. Here Seth portrays women who push against those old stereotypes through virtue of their intelligence and social power while also depicting himself as a man so consumed by his male-centered world

of comics that he inevitably drives any woman, *all* women, away. According to literary analyst Katie Mullins, *It's a Good Life*'s indirect, but ever-present, focus on gender "recalls attempts in comics history, particularly in the feminist movement starting in

---

86 A fictional author mentioned amongst such prominent real authors (and with such convincing backstory and supplementary materials) that readers may come to believe he is real. He's not. Kalo's as fictional as Santa Claus or Abraham Lincoln.

Seth uses graceful linework to evoke the comics of *The New Yorker*.

the sixties, to engage with political and social issues."[87]

It's a Good Life's artistic styling harkens back to *The New Yorker* comics Seth obsesses over. He uses thick lines to create cartoonish characters and impressive landscapes. Seth shaded his pages through a mix of black, white, and blue against yellowed paper, and his hand-written, perfectly imperfect lettering gives this retro-infused story a more intimate feel.

Seth's view of the world is intelligent, but at times myopic, introspective to the point of aggravating the reader with its self-importance, yet Seth sees his own shortcomings and comments on them. He also comments on how commenting on them isn't fixing them.

It's a Good Life, If You Don't Weaken obsesses over the medium of comics, managing to simultaneously be selfish, self-loathing, and introspective, managing to create a stylish commentary on the limitations of an overly-nostalgic perspective.

87 Mullins, Katie. *"Questioning Comics: Women and Autocritique in Seth's It's A Good Life, If You Don't Weaken."* Canadian Literature, (203), 11–27.

HICKSVILLE

Written by/art by: Dylan Horrocks
Published by: Black Eye Productions, 1988; Drawn and Quarterly, 2014 (reissue edition)

In *Hicksville*, everyone's a comic book expert, from the lady walking her dog to the guy running the hardware store. If you want to talk about the impact Jack Kirby had on the industry, or when, exactly, the "silver" age of comics ended and why, *Hicksville* is the place for you.

Journalist Leonard Batts travels to this elusive locale for answers about Rick Berger, the comics' industry new golden boy (who also happens to hail from Hicksville). On his journey he meets a cartoonist named Sam and the two of them explore the past and present of comics.

In the '90s, Image Comics was rising to the top of the industry with its combination of creator-owned properties and "mature" storytelling. At the time, many comics creators saw Image and its ilk as the death of comics, telling meaningless, shortsighted stories and milking fans of as much money as possible, over-emphasizing the idea of "collecting" over "enjoying" and leading to the eventual comics crash of the mid-to-late nineties. Fictional Rick Burger acts as a stand-in for many of the pompous creators of the day; any semblance of artistic vision he had was sacrificed long ago in the name of fame and fortune. Sam, on the other hand, sticks to making things he cares about, constantly battling self-doubt, writer's block, and poverty to produce content with a message he feels proud of.

Hicksville examines the history of the comics genre through conversations with its numerous characters, all inexplicable experts in the field. Horrocks' writing is charming and his art has a Don Martin-esque quality to it, preventing *Hicksville* from feeling too much like a straightforward history lesson.

Hicksville presents comics with both optimism and melancholy. For decades the medium was a

"THE OFFICIAL HISTORY OF COMICS IS A HISTORY OF FRUSTRATION, OF UNREALIZED POTENTIAL."
—KUPE, LIGHTHOUSE KEEPER

In Hicksville, everyone's a comics historian.

lonely, niche format beloved by a select few and largely ignored by the general public. Now, thanks to webcomics, online ordering, and the spread of nerd/geek culture, comics are more popular than ever, with traditional superhero stories and other, more offbeat works finally getting some of the recognition they've always deserved.

THE NAO OF BROWN
Written by/art by: Glyn Dillon
Published by: Harry N. Abrams; 2012

The Nao of Brown provides a gorgeous, flawed, look into Obsessive-Compulsive Disorder through half-Japanese, half-British woman, Nao Brown, the imperfect protagonist of an imperfect story.

It's rare to find stories about mental illness; unfortunately, there's too much stigma still attached to mental illness by the general public for publishers and producers to feel comfortable to create stories about them, and as long as this short-sighted mentality continues, the erasure of this stigma will be a slow and arduous process.

Nao's OCD manifests itself as violent fantasies about the people around her, fantasies which become increasingly potent as she becomes stressed, and the only way for her to alleviate these tendencies are through ritualistic thoughts and behaviors. On her way to mental health, Nao meets Gregory, a well-read, but drunken and asanine washing machine repairman, and falls inexplicably in love with him despite the fact that he mostly comes across as a complete jackass. Little does Nao know that her good friend and coworker, Steve, has been in love with her the entire time. Were it not for Nao's Obsessive-Compulsive Disorder, this would resemble a pretty standard romcom.

Dillon's art is jaw-droppingly gorgeous; intricate details litter every scene, phenomenal watercolors bloom across the page, and Dillon's magnificent art brings his characters to spectacular life. The actual story, however well-intentioned, does raise some problems. It presents OCD through too narrow a lens, too often avoiding the guilt and anxiety of being a functioning, intelligent person whose obsessive thoughts and compulsive behaviors feel so uncontrollable. Dillon ultimately seems to portray the disorder as being something in control of the person who has it (spoiler alert: mental illness isn't always something a person can control alone). Narratively, it's implied that Nao is being selfish for being too absorbed by her OCD to notice the problems of those around her, which is a dismissive, reductionist way of thinking. Also, despite Nao being ostensibly the main character, she is, as a charming, smart, beautiful woman, the manic pixie dream foil for Gregory and Steve to pursue. This portrayal cheapens both the story and mental illness alike. These problems are somewhat subtle, and may not be apparent to casual readers, but they're there.

Still, despite its flaws, *The Nao of Brown* acts as a good conversation starter for the infrequency with which mental illness is depicted in popular culture, and its art is nothing short of spectacular.

"I WAS PLEASED THAT I'D HAD SUCH A NORMAL THOUGHT, BUT IT STILL DIDN'T FEEL RIGHT. WHAT AM I DOING? I SHOULD NEVER FLY."
-NAO BROWN

Dillon often uses a striking red to draw the reader's eye to Nao.

SHORTCOMINGS

Written by/art by: Adrian Tomine • Published by: Drawn and Quarterly, 2007; reprint edition, 2009

Ben's got a problem with something. Ben's got a problem with a *lot* of things, actually. He's one of the most negative characters ever put to print, relentlessly pessimistic about everything. This was dumb, that is probably stupid, that city is terrible … he's so negative, he can't even take thanks for performing a simple act of kindness ("What else was I going to do?" he responds). Ben's biggest problem, though, is his perspective on Asian people, an unacknowledged (by him) racism, which permeates his being. He thinks white guys who go for Asian women are acting out some sort of pedophilic fantasy, yet Asian men (like him) who go for white girls are okay.

Like *American-Born Chinese, Shortcomings* ruminates on the unspoken self-loathing felt by much of the Asian-American population. As always, Tomine has a knack for writing dialogue that flows naturally, crafting realistic characters who are each superb in their mundanity, and here he uses straightforward panel layouts and artistic direction to let his characters do the talking.

Ben's girlfriend, Miko, is an intelligent, active young woman heavily involved in the Asian-

Ben fails to recognize his shortcomings.

"MAN... LOOK AT ALL THESE ASIANS!"
–BEN TANAKA

American community. She's also got her own issues to deal with while Ben ignores his problems; scenes featuring the two of them buzz with potential energy as their relationship slowly works toward its inevitable outcome. In many ways, Miko seems to be the more standard protagonist—she grows and changes over the course of *Shortcomings.* Ben, meanwhile, refuses to. Tomine's smart dialogue makes it easy to stay interested in this static protagonist, though, even as his story arc continues moving and he selfishly, cravenly rejects moving along with it.

The journey within a story is often worth going on because it allows the audience to experience the protagonist's change over time. Generally it's a change for the better, but sometimes it's a change for the worse. Other times, however, the protagonist refuses to change, never yielding to thematic forces pressuring them to become someone else in order to survive. In the case of Ben Tanaka, *Shortcomings* gives him every chance to recognize his own issues and act accordingly, yet he continues barreling forward, approaching insight while always looking away at the last moment to avoid self-reflection.

Shortcomings offers a look into the complexities of being an Asian-American without the easy out of cloying feel-goodery or sweeping philosophical statements; it's a slice of life story focused on presenting a small, normal truth.

GHOST WORLD

Written by/art by: Daniel Clowes
Published by: Fantagraphics; 2001

Be forewarned, dear reader. If you are coming into *Ghost World* expecting supernaturally themed japes and escapades, you'll be sorely disappointed. The only ghosts here are metaphorical as faux-intellectual snarkypants best friends, Rebecca and Enid, haunt their home town as post-high school phantoms.

GHOST WORLD
Daniel Clowes

Rebecca and Enid like to play the part of counter-cultural hipsters, mocking strangers in snide little asides meant to make each other laugh and prove their superiority. Enid's more aggressive in her mockery—as the loud-mouthed member of the duo she says almost anything that pops into her head, regardless of how it makes someone else feel. She's also prone to lying to make herself sound more interesting. Rebecca, on the other hand, is a bit more subdued, yet she's so attached to Enid that the thought of her going off to college and leaving her behind terrifies her. They have a sad sort of friendship, acting as if they are

each other's only friends because everyone else is beneath them, when, really, they may only be friends because they're the only people who *want* to be friends with them.

Clowes' writing shines sharply throughout *Ghost World*. Enid and Rebecca's rambling conversation hop from topic to topic with effortless naturality; you get a quick sense of their character while still getting a sense that they're trying to feel out who, *exactly* their characters are. The battle between seemingly-

dull normalcy and intellectually-superior misfit-ism pervades the book; much like Daria Morgendorffer and Jane Lane of *Daria,* Enid and Rebecca rebel loudly against the status quo, primarily by standing off to the side and making snide quips about everything. Unlike Daria and Jane, however, Enid and Rebecca are just as, if not more, phony, self-centered, impressionable, and naive as the people they're making fun of, and lack the introspectiveness necessary to make any sort of changes.

THE PROPERTY

Written by/art by: Rutu Modan • Published by: Drawn and Quarterly; 2013

In *Back to the Future*, Marty McFly travels back in time to the 1950s, to an era wherein his parents are the same age as him. In the past, his parents

are full of the same hopes, dreams, and hormones he is. They're youthful, bright-eyed, and looking to the future—a stark contrast to the beat-down, sad sacks he's come to pity. It's baffling to him to see his folks from this new light, getting to understand them as equals, rather than as parents. In *The Property*, Mica Segal travels to Warsaw with her grandmother to deal with a property dispute, and in doing so she, like Marty, learns more about her grandparents than she ever knew existed.

Dual messages of discovery and love lost pervade *The Property*. Modan takes us through an exploration of European cultures, showing broad,

Mica and Gram-Gram don't always see eye to eye.

> ""WITH FAMILY, YOU DON'T HAVE TO TELL THE WHOLE TRUTH AND IT'S NOT CONSIDERED LYING."
> -RUTU MODAN

intercultural conflicts and biases while telling a story that's small and familial. Modan expertly uses body language to convey the emotions of her characters; few artists pack as much nuance into the paralinguistic cues of human interactions as she does.

Mica and her grandmother serve as the primary propulsion for the story with both their relationship and relationships. The interactions between these two shifts in every direction—at times they're talkative, silent, angry, concerned, bewildered, and loving, often simultaneously. Memorable characters populate *The Property*'s many pages, but it's Gramma Regina and Mica who'll keep you turning pages, wanting to know what they're going to do next, trying to find the next development in Mica's young life or the next tale of Regina's star-crossed past.

SWALLOW ME WHOLE

Written by/art by: Nate Powell
Published by: Top Shelf Productions; 2008

According to Smithsonian.com, a whale shark can't swallow you whole—its esophagus is too small. A sperm whale could, however, and it might just do it, so keep an eye on any sperm whales you see. *Swallow Me Whole* by Nate Powell, isn't about sharks or whales, though, it's about a topic rarely explored in popular culture—mental illness.[88]

Swallow Me Whole features two step-siblings, Ruth and Perry, both struggling with schizophrenia-induced hallucinations. They recognize the things they see are indeed figments conjured by their brains, but that doesn't stop them from conversing with and carrying out demands from the hallucinations. Ruth and Perry both fight to appear normal;  as the story progresses and adolescence kicks in, their paths diverge as their conditions are exacerbated based on societal/gender standards.

When Ruth starts behaving aggressively by talking back to her teachers and raising her voice, she's immediately taken to a doctor, diagnosed with schizophrenia and obsessive-compulsive disorder, and medicated accordingly. Perry, on the other hand, tries to reach out to a doctor about his hallucinations, but is blown off because the only thing the

88 Powell explains that the idea for this graphic novel came to him in a "powerful dream." He doesn't go into further detail about the dream, so one can safely assume it was about sperm whales. Quote retrieved from: http://blog.tfaw.com/2010/08/25/nate-powell-on-swallow-me-whole-mental-illness-the-magic-of-siblings/.

hallucinations want him to do is draw things, which is deemed a socially-appropriate activity.

Ruth's hallucinations, primarily consisting of insects, grow worse over the course of the story. These imaginary swarms obey her beck and call, giving her the sweet freedom of control she's lacking in her day-to-day life. Powell excels at illustrating these eerie hallucinations, using an entire realm of color despite the black-and-white format, and his gift for portraying emotion brings a rawness to every panel.

Swallow Me Whole opens a window into the world of mental illness from the perspective of the affected. Powell foregoes creating a happy, clean story to make something more strange, more unnerving, more *surprising*.

Swallow Me Whole's sharp storytelling highlights the problems with gender stereotypes and the stigma of mental illness. Anyone who has ever suffered mental illness, or who knows someone who has, will likely find that this story hits close to home, and for anyone else it will serve as an elucidating look into the problems of gender stereotypes and the stigmatization of mental health issues.

Ruth's hallucinations really bug her.

BEHIND THE INK: NATE POWELL

Nate Powell pulls double-duty as both writer and artist, producing graphic novels on his own as well as being highly sought after for his fierce artistic skills.

At fourteen he began self-publishing his own comics,

which helped pave the way to his becoming an award-winning *New York Times* bestselling graphic novelist, snagging prestigious recognition such as an Eisner Award and a Robert F. Kennedy Book Award.

Powell bears the ability to produce captivating stories through thoughtful writing and creative imagery, often using heavy inking to create dark, yet expressive, imagery, and utilizing jarring juxtapositions for enhanced effects. For example, in *March*, Powell contrasts images of a riot's aftermath with images of a woman singing, "My Country, 'Tis of Thee" at President Obama's inauguration. As she sings, "Let freedom ring," a series of small panels depicts men celebrating the hate-fueled violence they inflicted, a confederate flag flying brazenly, lifeless bodies in the street, and a child looking forlorn at his fingers—fingers he just used to gouge a person's eyes out.

PROMINENT WORKS:
• *Swallow Me Whole* (2008)
• *Any Empire* (2011)
• *The Silence of Our Friends* (2012)
• *March* (2013)

UNLIKELY
Written by/art by: Jeffrey Brown
Published by: Top Shelf Productions; 2003

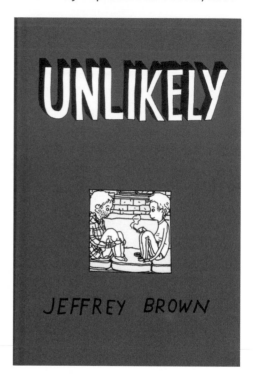

Jeffrey Brown's autobiographical tale depicts his time as a naive twenty-something navigating the complexities of his first relationship. *Unlikely* isn't an epic tale, nor is it beautiful, but it's an honest one.

Brown chronicles his relationship with Allisyn, his first major girlfriend, a woman who is much more experienced than he but not necessarily more worldly. Jeff, on the other hand, is a virgin. He's sweet, sort of spineless, and sexually repressed. Getting to know Allisyn is, for him, a long and time-intensive process.

Set during the '90s, *Unlikely* shows us the early stages of Jeff and Allisyn's relationship. Playing voice tag on the answering machine,[89] non-committal responses to see what the other thinks first, subtle movements as they cross the body language boundary between "friends" and "more than friends." Heavy topics and philosophical musings are rarely explored; rather, *Unlikely* lingers on more mundane, real-life moments. Brown takes his time with this story. Taken individually, most scenes are normal to the point of banality, but together they add up to depict a relationship as it grows and intertwines, blooms, and eventually wilts. Brown's rough art style gives the sketchy feeling of notes in a diary, with simple facial expressions and sloppy backgrounds depicting the essence, rather than the actuality, of each moment.

89 For those of you who were too young to make phone calls in the '90s, first, we should explain that an answering machine is a device that you could send text messages to, only they were texts made out of your voice, and secondly, you're going to have to write the rest of this book yourself because we're going to be too busy digging our old asses some early graves.

Allisyn, you go, girl! There's another blast from the '90s for ya.

THE STORY OF MY TITS

Written by/art by: Jennifer Hayden • Published by: Top Shelf Productions; 2015

All mammals have mammary glands and nipples. In Jennifer Hayden's debut graphic novel, *The Story of My Tits,* she enlightens us to the story of her mammary glands. Hayden turns the story of these glands into a fetching account of their entire lifespan. "I was born without any tits," she states. "Just the usual one-size fits-all nipples. Because of this, I was happy and stupid and free."[90] She continues with how she came to realize the world would expect more from her breasts, the anguish of waiting for her breasts to fill out, the love for them once they did, and the grieving process when facing a double mastectomy due to breast cancer. Despite covering the deadly-serious topic of breast cancer, *The Story of My Tits* isn't a dire tale, nor is it solely focused on the life-threatening disease. Hayden explains, "I set out to tell a survivor's story that would be the story of a woman, and the last chapter is cancer, not a cancer story per se."

Hayden's wit, sarcasm, and knack for off-beat metaphors are used to freely discuss both her body in general and breasts in specific, giving the book a conspiratorial feel, as if you're Hayden's good friend sharing stories with her over drinks and food. Hayden states that humor has always been part of her life, so it was a necessary part of her book: "My husband and I both have kind of gallows humor. Humor had to be part of this book because it was such an underlying part of this story. That's the

"SOMEBODY HAS TO HAVE A BAD BIOPSY. WHY NOT ME?"
—JENNIFER HAYDEN

healing, when you start to laugh." [91]

All in all, *The Story of My Tits* is motivational and cathartic, insightful into the triumphs and turbulence of life while also acting as an exceptional piece of educational literature about the struggles a woman goes through when combating breast cancer.

---

90 Jennifer Hayden, *The Story of My Tits.*

91 Quotes retrieved from: http://www.publishersweekly.com/pw/by-topic/industry-news/comics/article/68648-jennifer-hayden-tells-the-story-of-my-tits.html.

Momma doesn't feel like chatting right now, dear, so SOD OFF!

Philosophy and English majors, rejoice. *Asterios Polyp* is here for you; this seemingly-straightforward tale of a man's path to redemption comes jam-packed with highbrow conversations regarding immortality, duality, metaknowledge, free will, and more.

The titular Asterios Polyp's life is in shambles, partly as a result of his own hubris, and partly because of a freak lightning bolt. He leaves his life as a tenured, respected professor of architecture behind, opting to move to a new town and become a mechanic's assistant as part of his quest to better himself. We meet Asterios at his lowest and David Mazzucchelli takes us back and forth through time to show us how he got there, where he's going, and where his twin brother, Ignazio, might have gone had he not died in the womb.

Nontraditional layouts abound in *Asterios Polyp;* Mazzucchelli uses unconventional techniques to convey emotion and signify meaning through his art. Asterios was, for most of his life, a pompous ass, constantly talking over everyone, especially his longtime lover and wife, Hana, a brilliant artist lacking the confidence to push back against his ego. Mazzucchelli signifies each major character with different colors, showing shifting ratios of these hues as power dynamics shift throughout the story. It's one of the many clever techniques used throughout *Asterios Polyp* which uses the medium of sequential art to its fullest extent.

Asterios and his many conversational

partners are all marvelously well-read (except for the mechanic Stiffly, whose lack of formal education and propensity for mixing metaphors are as obvious as the nose on a fish needing a bicycle). These conversations cover a wide bevy of topics; when paired with *Asterios Polyp*'s occasional dreamlike sequences ripe with symbolic imagery, you've got a book eager for repeated readings and in-depth analyses.

AND WHEN HE CAME OVER TO INTRODUCE HIMSELF,

I'M SORRY. MY NAME'S ASTERIOS POLYP.

SHE FELT SHE WAS STARING STRAIGHT INTO THE SPOTLIGHT.

As Asterios and Hana mingle socially, so, too, do their colors.

THE VOYEURS

Written by/art by: Gabrielle Bell • Published by: Uncivilized Books; 2012

The Voyeurs opens with a literal enactment of its title—a group of people hanging out on a roof top entranced at the sight of a couple having sex across

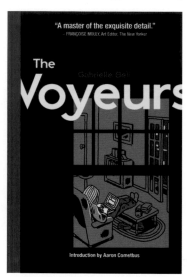

the street from them. Windows open, unashamed, this couple is fully engrossed in the passion of the moment ... until they realize that a group of weirdos is gawking at them; then they close the curtains. So goes *The Voyeurs*, Gabrielle Bell's melancholy autobiographical tale of a five-year period of her life.

Bell is unflinchingly honest in depicting her own thoughts (or seems to be, anyway, since she's the only person who *truly* knows if she is being honest). During the period depicted in *The Voyeurs*, Bell traveled abroad, promoted a movie, met lots of new people, encountered adoring fans, and generally had what most would consider a good time. To Bell, however, these times are uncomfortable, often leaving her feeling detached and unworthy. Despite having a considerable bibliography at that point in her life, Bell seems to still be feeling the effects

of Imposter Syndrome—an inability to internalize your own accomplishments and the consistent fear that you will be "found out" as a fraud.[92] Bell's mood vacillates from page to page, her narration often disconnected from the actions of the panels. Bell might be receiving accolades at San Diego Comic-Con, but in her head she's wondering if the compliments were meant for someone else, praying for the moment she can leave the public eye and be alone again with her misery. Rather than conveying an obvious plotline throughout the book, Bell's story is of an internal journey through the ins and outs of her various neuroses, one richly decorated with moments and people from her life captured in a way that feels genuine. *The Voyeurs* is a frank look at the miseries we all keep tucked away, of suffering quietly, and of feeling detached from the people and events populating your life.

"As she watches other people living life, and watches herself watching them, Bell's pen becomes a kind of laser, first illuminating the surface distractions of the world, then scorching them away to reveal a deeper reality that is almost too painful and too beautiful to bear."—Alison Bechdel, author of *Fun Home.*[93]

---

92 Clance, P.R.; Imes, S.A. (1978). "The imposter phenomenon in high achieving women: dynamics and therapeutic intervention.". Psychotherapy: Theory, Research and Practice 15 (3): 241–247.

93 *Voyeurs* (back cover) by Gabrielle Bell.

"LATELY, I'VE REALIZED THAT WHENEVER I'M HUGGED,
I RETREAT SOMEWHERE INSIDE MYSELF AND WAIT FOR IT TO BE OVER."
—GABRIELLE BELL

Bell suffers through the hell of intimacy.

THE SCULPTOR

Written by/art by: Scott McCloud • Published by First Second; 2015

Tortured young artist David Smith has had a rough life. His parents are both dead (dad in a car crash, mom to cancer) and his chronically ill sister passed away recently. As a twenty-six-year-old sculptor living in New York City, David *has* to leave his mark on the world, yet no matter how hard he tries, he just can't seem to break through. When the spirit of Death, under the friendly guise of David's uncle, offers him the power to sculpt *anything* (in exchange for David agreeing to die in 200 days), David accepts. Yet, even with this unlimited artistic power David struggles to break into the art world which shunned him, and his artistic misdirections only grow more complicated when he falls in love with the free-spirited Meg— a relationship that's doomed from the start, seeing as how David's scheduled to punch his ticket off the mortal coil pretty soon.

The Sculptor represents the many ways we try to create a legacy, whether it's through artistic creations, experiential richness, social connections, or raising offspring. David is locked into that struggle to make a name for himself—a struggle exacerbated by the fact that there's another *much* more famous

sculptor named David Smith. It doesn't help that David lives by a rigidly obstinate set of principles— principles which hinder him while the more flexible people around him find easier paths to success and happiness. McCloud crafts intelligent, beautiful panels, often using unconventional techniques such as depicting a sidewalk into a calendar to illustrate David's slow walk toward his inevitable demise, or blending multicultural comic influences to grant greater energy and gravitas to a scene.

Both David Smith's sculpting ability and *The Sculptor* in general speak to the pain of being an artist, to have an idea that burns so hot inside of you that you struggle to bring it out in the same, perfect, shape you envisioned it in. This tragic tale of artistry, of time wasted and time cherished, will push readers to find satisfaction in their own lives, whether it's by relishing what they do have or by finally finding the discipline to reach inside themselves and rip out that burning, beautiful idea for the world to see, imperfections and all.

There's only so much future ahead of us, but if you can slow down to appreciate the present, you'll find

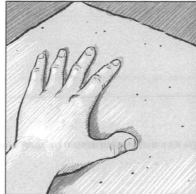

David gets to work.

that it can stretch on for near-infinity.

"*The slowing of [The Sculptor's] pace is a way of evoking the whole idea of acceptance. Y'know, you feel like you're racing the clock, as [David] does for much of the story, and finally he comes to appreciate how much can be unpacked from each and every minute by living in the present. And the best way to show that is to unpack those minutes and allow them to spread across a greater amount of space. The story slows because his heartbeat is finally slowing. He's finally allowing each day to grow to its full size by mindfully enjoying every aspect of those days.*"[94] —Scott McCloud

94 Quote retrieved from: comicsalliance.com/research-references-and-structuring-stories-scott-mccloud-goes-in-depth-on-the-sculptor-interview/.

KILLING AND DYING

Written by/art by: Adrian Tomine • Published by: Drawn & Quarterly; 2015

It's a difficult thing to capture the essence of a life. Writers, artists, singers, all search their souls for that bit of truth that shines a light on themselves and reflects onto others. With Adrian Tomine's *Killing and Dying,* we get a collection of several short stories presenting some of the most truthful depictions of life put to page. Tomine's stories are intimate, mundane in their content, and sublime in their execution.

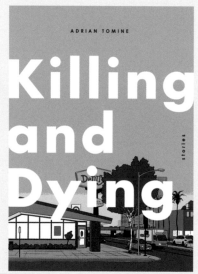

Hortisculpture centers around Harold—husband, father, gardener. After reading a magazine, he gets the idea to combine plants and pottery to create living art. Most everyone is uninterested in his idea, at best, and a few even draw disparaging comparisons to Chia Pets. Only his wife supports him, but Harold's own neuroses prevent him from accepting her support; instead he blames her for "puffing him up" into believing he could actually make something of himself. Harold highlights that quest which so many of us go through: the quest to do something bigger, better, more *fulfilling* than what we already have, and, like many people, Harold's own shortcomings keep him from finding that fulfillment there.

Abuse takes many forms, and in *Go Owls*, it takes the insidious form of a seemingly-loving boyfriend who "just wants to take care of" his girlfriend. His abuse is random; one moment he'll be laughing with her, the next he'll demean her to her very soul or beat her with a shoe. He isolates his girlfriend, insisting she only talk on the phone when he is around (and, curiously, only talk to him on the phone, defeating the whole purpose), and constantly wraps his arm around her in a show of ownership.

Comedians, like any field, have their own peculiar vernacular. If you do well on stage, it's said that you "killed," and if your jokes aren't landing, it's said that you "died." In *Killing and Dying,* the short story bearing the same name as the collection, a frugal, pessimistic father tries desperately to support and connect with his daughter while his cancer-ridden wife caters to their teenage child's every whim.

Like all of Tomine's work, *Killing and Dying* comes loaded with masterfully laid out panels detailing the little things, changes in expression, stuttered speech, and fleeting moments between moments that bring the human experience to life. *Killing and Dying, Go Owl, Hortisculpture,* and the many other stories contained in this collection all use similar, but varied, artistic styles to tell their tales. *The Intruders* uses a monochromatic color scheme to illustrate its protagonist's isolation. *Translated from the Japanese*

What a jerk.

is written in second-person, drawn in first-person. *Hortisculpture* pays homage to newspaper comics with four-panel sequences laid out as if there's a punchline at the end (often misleading us when the punchline is instead something pitiful) and with occasional pages fully-colored in a pointillistic style *a la* newspaper printing.

Tomine's work on *Killing and Dying* moves from story to story with measured pace, planting wonderfully normal details within each tale that all grow together to form the larger picture of people who are broken, people who are hopeful, and people who

are, more than anything, human.

"*I think most cartoonists are solitary, lonely kids who use their work as a way to try to connect with the world. If I had any other skills that were more performative—if I could have been a musician or an actor—I'm sure I would have pursued that instead in order to get that instant feedback and to hear applause. I think drawing my weird little mini-comics for twenty people in Sacramento was my completely mutated version of that.*"[95] —Adrian Tomine

95 *Retrieved from: https://www.guernicamag.com/interviews/drawing-from-life-and-death/.*

A father tries his best to connect to his daughter.

BEHIND THE INK: ADRIAN TOMINE

Our adolescent years come with a storm of self-doubts, self-transformation, and all kinds of bodily weirdness. At age sixteen, writer/artist Adrian Tomine boldly put his metamorphosis on display by creating his comic series, *Optic Nerve*, which is magically still going to this day.

Much of that longevity can be attributed to Tomine's success as an observer of the human condition—one whose perspective is ever-shifting. When asked about *Optic Nerve*'s long life, he replied, "When I first started drawing the earliest incarnation of *Optic Nerve*, I hadn't even been on a date; I hadn't had a romantic relationship of any kind yet, so in a way, I was almost writing science fiction. It was my pathetic version of trying to imagine what the future might be like! Now I'm forty years old and I'm married with two kids, and I live on the opposite side of the country, so I probably can't help but bring a different perspective to the work."

Tomine uses a clean-line art style strongly influenced by artists such as Jaime Hernandez and Dan Clowes. His writing comes with a distinctively open-endedness to it, often with minimal thought balloons or narration to leave the reader to interpret things as they want. This open-endedness is a deliberate move on Tomine's part.

"Some of the story hinges on believing in the reality of it," said Tomine, "that if someone is sitting silently in a chair, they're not just sitting there completely brain-dead, that there is stuff happening internally that we as the observer don't have access to."[96]

PROMINENT WORKS:
- *32 Stories: The Complete Optic Nerve Mini-Comics* (1998)
- *Summer Blonde* (2002)
- *Shortcomings* (2007)
- *Killing and Dying* (2015)

96 Quotes retrieved from: http://www.believermag.com/issues/200710/?read=interview_tomine.

CHAPTER 7

THE #1 *NEW YORK TIMES* BEST-SELLING CLASSIC

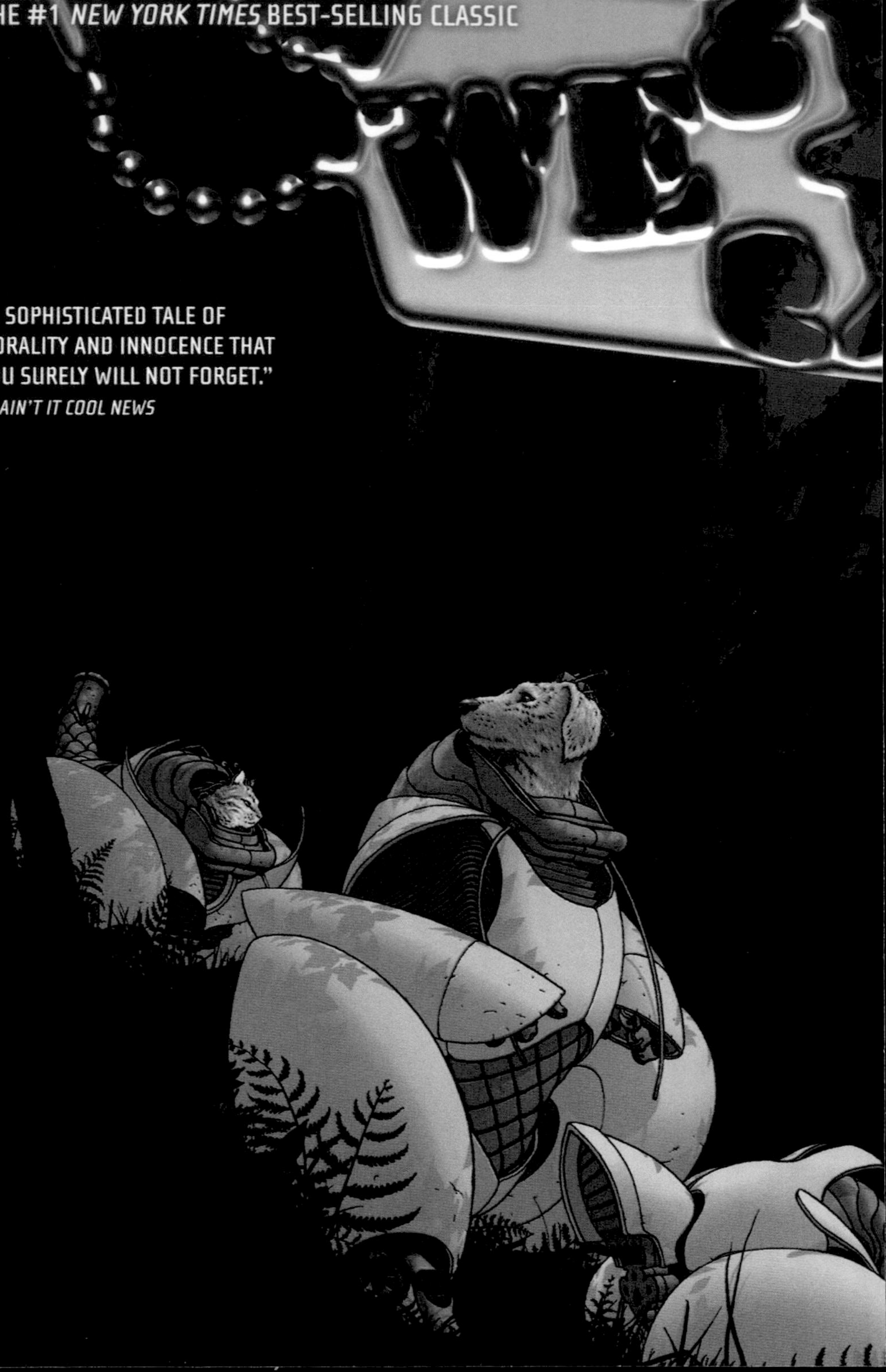

"A SOPHISTICATED TALE OF MORALITY AND INNOCENCE THAT YOU SURELY WILL NOT FORGET."
— *AIN'T IT COOL NEWS*

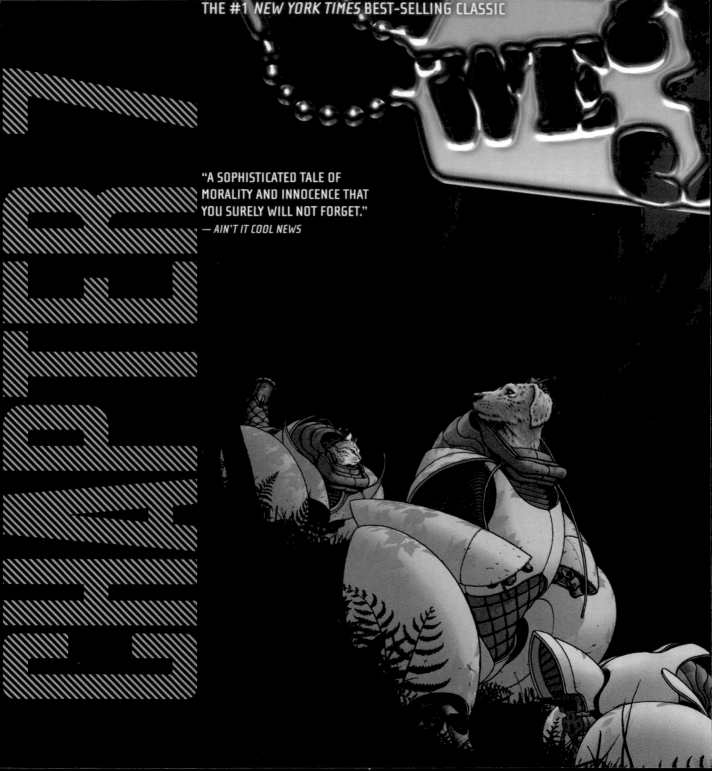

ODDS AND ENDS: THE ICONOCLASTS

///////////////////////

Alternative comics have often laughed at the mainstream, telling stories that are bizarre, unparalleled, and entirely unique. Which makes their brilliant works hard to sort when you're organizing works by genre; thusly, we built this chapter as much out of respect as out of necessity. There are books which absolutely, positively *must* be included in any discussion of the greatest graphic novels, yet for whatever reason, they defy categorization.

In the case of *WE3* and other similar tales, it's here because we didn't make a science-fiction or cuddly-animal-friends chapter (not that *WE3* is particularly cuddly).

In the case of *The Acme Novelty Library* and its ilk, it's because they thumb their nose at convention so hard that their noses come flying off to smack you in the face, and when you look back at them, they've got a second nose ready to be thumbed off, only this one is blue and screaming about taxes. These stories delight in being deviant, and we delight in their deviancy.

THE FRANK BOOK

Written by/art by: Jim Woodring • Published by: Fantagraphic Books; 2003

What is Frank, exactly? A dog? A cat? Some kind of stub-toothed walrus man? Who knows. Frank, like the rest of the world he lives in, is a bit of a mysterious weirdo, and *The Frank Book* chronicles his life in a world of mind-bending surreality.

Frank's a naturally curious fellow, and his short, detached vignettes are full of plenty to be curious about. Misshapen creatures, interdimensional beings, geometrically-shaped chickens, and a Manhog populate his surroundings. Frank's most loyal ally is his pet/best friend, Pupshaw, a triangular creature with a broad face, tiny stub legs, and a raccoon tail. Pupshaw's constantly bailing out the hapless Frank from whatever trouble he gets himself into (or, at the very least, warning him before he gets into said trouble). Frank's escapades brazenly ignore continuity from one story to the next, and while they sometimes contain lessons for those willing to look deeply enough into the madness, sometimes, the lesson seems to *be* madness.

In one of Frank's more salient outings, he receives an invitation to a Palace of Horrors. Always in search of a good scare, Frank eagerly hurries toward the Palace. On the way he encounters grotesque sights—creatures torturing each other, a humanoid slicing portions of his own face off, etc. Once he reaches the Palace of Horrors, he finds its gentle spookery unstimulating. On his return trip he passes, again, by the real-world horrors, and upon returning home he labels his entrance "exit," implying that the real world is where the truest horrors lay.

Manhog, a grotesque, beady-eyed human/porcine hybrid, suffers most frequently in this bizarre land, frequently ending up maimed or dead by the end of a story. Manhog is cruel and cowardly—antagonistic, but not really an antagonist—and with his selfish nature and misshapen body, he is a damned soul forever trapped in a phantasmagorical hellscape.

With Frank's world, Woodring has created a place utterly fantastic and terrible to behold, with stories which manage to be complex without ever relying on the spoken word. Woodring alternates between gorgeous, soft coloring and black-and-white stories; regardless of which chromatic style he chooses, the result is always crystal-clear and gorgeous in its own bizarre way. Woodring creates creatures which are dreamy and swirling, yet often with a distinct geometric base to them for easy visual identification. His backgrounds are generally comprised of normal scenes of nature and odd, but not altogether alien, buildings. Woodring uses wavy lines to convey both

mood and a sense of otherness to every scene, so even when things are normal, they're not *that* normal.

The Frank Book serves as a window into something captivatingly strange, often inexplicable, and unquestionably fantastic.

"*All of the Frank stories have straightforward meanings which I usually recognize only after they are drawn and printed. I used to explain these meanings to anyone who asked, but I've stopped doing that because the stories are more powerful when their mysteries are undiscovered.*" -Jim Woodring[97]

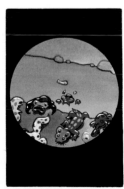

Frank spots trouble. Lots of it.

WIMBLEDON GREEN: THE GREATEST COMIC BOOK COLLECTOR IN THE WORLD

Written by/art by: Seth • Published by: Drawn & Quarterly; 2005

Surely you've heard of Wimbledon Green, the greatest comic book collector ever to grace the scene? No one's sure who he really is (though all the experts have their theories) nor where he got his money, but it's hard to argue against the impressiveness of the man's collection, his knowledge, or appreciation of the comics art form. Through this mysterious protagonist, Seth examines both the comics industry and the perspective of collectors, ruminating on why we treasure the things we do.

Set in a Canadian present-future-past complete with rocket cars and high-tech radio surveillance, *Wimbledon Green* tells the tale of Wimbledon's quest to obtain *The Green Ghost #1*, a legendary comic book, as well as the history of the Webb Collection, a mythical pile of priceless antique comics. The story often cuts to "interviews" with other comic book collectors speaking of the eponymous comics historian. Some are clearly jealous, some are *subtly* jealous, and others appreciate this man's appreciation of

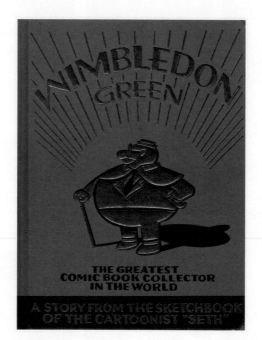

the thing they, too, love so very much. While many interviewees get featured throughout Wimbledon Green, many get repeat appearances, often to place greater emphasis on whichever stereotype or character flaw they represent. Collectors are a funny bunch, muses *Wimbledon Green,* often amassing their treasures out of a nostalgia for their simpler pasts, or for pasts they never actually got to have. *Wimbledon Green* gently pokes fun at comics historians/collectors, but never outright mocks them; these jokes, these stereotypical characters, all come from a place of appreciation.

Seth utilizes an old-timey art style here, with simple characters similar to what you'd find in early comics (only with much cleaner linework). Many panels are scrunched little things packed with dialogue, giving the feeling of passionate nerds breathlessly rambling about the things they love and obsess over.

"WHO WAS WIMBLEDON GREEN? HE BURST ON THE SCENE FULLY FORMED—OUT OF NOWHERE—AND LATER, HE DISAPPEARED JUST AS QUICKLY."
—DANNY, OF MORE FUN COMICS & CARDS

THE ACME NOVELTY LIBRARY

Written by/art by: Chris Ware • Published by: Pantheon Books, 2005; and Fantagraphic Books

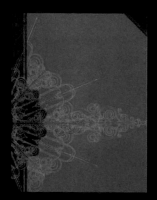

From the moment you pick up the book, it's clear that *The Acme Novelty Library* has no interest in holding your hand through a straightforward narrative. Its cover bears no title, nor author credit, and the content begins on the very first page—there's no copyright material, no blank pages, no thank yous, *nothing*. *The Acme Novelty Library* has a lot to say, and by God, it's going to say it.

The Acme Novelty Library primarily makes use of two presentational styles. Firstly, many pages bear huge, fake ads advertising services which don't exist. These faux ads advertise services to disconnect you from others, or to discourage you from having the "life-ruiner" that is children. These ads are, at their lightest, black comedy, and at their darkest they're damning indictments of our increasingly disconnected society.

The Acme Novelty Library also features huge comics reminiscent of archaic comics such as *The Katzenjammer Kids, Popeye,* and *Little Nemo.* Several storylines recur throughout the book with entries such as *Big Tex,* a rustic yokel

What's *really* going on here?

who can't seem to understand that his father hates him, or *Rusty Brown*, a selfish, collection-obsessed nerd cut off from the rest of the world. These tales feature splashy, eponymous titles and characters prone to distinctive drawls and self-talk. Unlike those early comics, however, these aren't built around wild adventures and wacky punchlines, but lonesome un-adventures and disheartening anti-comedy. Concepts like isolation, the all-consuming search for meaning, and the destructive powers of apathy and selfishness pervade *The Acme Novelty Library*. With its sly depth and massive pages filled with tiny panels and tinier fonts, this is a long journey well worth treading for comic enthusiasts eager to explore something vast and unique, or for anyone looking to wander off the beaten path for a while, unconcerned with whether or not they ever come back.

THE X'ED OUT TRILOGY:

X'ed Out, The Hive, and Sugar Skull • Written by/art by: Charles Burns
Published by: Pantheon, 2010 (X'ed Out); 2012 (The Hive); 2014 (Sugar Skull)

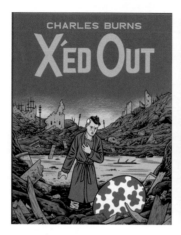  

Pig fetuses. Creepy Tintin masks. Douchebag lizard men. A hive full of women pregnant with giant speckled eggs. To anyone familiar with *Black Hole,* it should come as no surprise that its author would create a new story full of the bold and the bizarre.

Doug, a wannabe performance artist, is trying to remember what's going on with his life. He woke up in a strange desert world full of alien creatures, with flitting images of his past popping up to guide and confound him. What happened between him and Sarah? Why does he have this bandage on his head? What's the deal with the guy in the bathrobe? Doug struggles to understand this alien world while thinking back to his life in the "real" world to figure out where everything went horribly wrong.

A master of the unusual, Charles Burns often uses *non-sequitur*-style panel layouts, bounding around to seemingly unrelated images to convey both a sense of mood (and occasionally story) while leaving the reader deliberately perplexed, enticing you to read and think further to suss out meaning. Burns work here is akin to a fever dream; blurred, burning images half-remembered in a haze. His characters often have slack-jawed, beady-eyed expressions to belie both their lack of intelligence and mirror the confusion of the audience. Burns, with his extraordinarily clean

"OCCASIONALLY I'D GLANCE OUT THERE AND SEE SARAH WITH A SMILE ON HER FACE ... AND IT WASN'T A FAKE SMILE. IT WAS THE REAL THING."
—DOUG

Doug meets a cat in *Sugar Skull*.

art style, is no wanton artist; every deliberate little detail is easy to notice (even if their meaning isn't immediately clear). The *X'ed Out* trilogy's strange storyline and imagery may take time to arrive at meaning, but each throwaway, unintelligible line of dialogue, every seemingly random image, every panel and page are all working toward a precise end. Burns asks for trust from his audience and repays that trust with a fascinating finale.

"*Burns has the kind of sick, profuse imagination that Hieronymus Bosch had. This imaginative fertility produces a frisson of atavistic horror, playing on the same revulsion of sex and an attendant gynecological phobia that the mad Lear rails against: 'Beneath is all the fiends':/There's hell, there's darkness, there is the sulphurous pit,/ Burning, scalding, stench, consumption . . .'*" -Neel Mukherjee, author of *The Lives of Others*[98]

Doug finds himself in an alien world in *X'ed Out*.

---

98 Quote retrieved from: http://www.newstatesman.com/books/2014/10/fevers-and-mirrors-surreal-graphic-novels-charles-burns.

LOGICOMIX

Written by: Apostolos Doxiadis and Christos H. Papadimitriou • Art by: Alecos Papados and Annie Di Donna
Published by: Bloomsbury USA; 2009

Pacifist, philosopher, mathematician, and logician ... Bertrand Russell is inarguably one of history's greatest thinkers. *Logicomix* follows his life's journey from a young boy to a respected academician in an exploration of the concept of logic itself. It's a long, winding road full of many detours, and isn't for the faint of brain.

Logicomix flies through some of the largest mathematical/logical debates of the nineteenth and twentieth centuries, covering the works of such geniuses as Immanuel Kant, David Hume, Aristotle, Plato, Alan Turing, Kurt Godel, Ludwig Wittgenstein, and Alfred North Whitehead, just to name a few. Russell's life story contains some minor thematic moments—personal suffering mostly endured due to the hubris of great minds such as his—while mostly keeping the focus on high levels of thought.

Doxiadis et al frame Russell's story of exploring the concept of logic by presenting a fictionalized account of *Logicomix's* writing and art team debating the story's execution and meaning. *Logicomix* yearns to educate readers on heady topics, offering copious amounts of material for the academically-minded to absorb, research, and discuss.

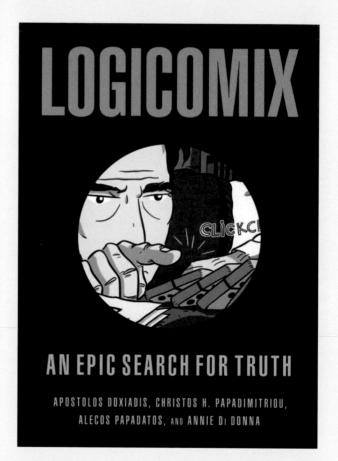

"MATHEMATICS IS THE LAST RECOURSE OF REASON!
WE CANNOT UNDERMINE IT WITH SLOPPY THINKING!"
—BERTRAND RUSSELL

I had a lot to put in it!

...THEREFORE, AS WE KNOW BY THE **PARALLEL POSTULATE**...

WHICH IS?

THE FACT THAT THROUGH A **POINT** OUTSIDE A LINE, ONLY **ONE** PARALLEL TO THE LINE PASSES.

BUT WE HAVEN'T YET PROVEN **THAT!**

If we can't trust math, what can we trust?

THAT'S BECAUSE IT IS AN **AXIOM**, MY LAD!

BUT YOU SAID IN GEOMETRY WE MUST PROVE **EVERYTHING** WE SAY!

WHAT'S THE VALUE OF A **PROOF** IF IT RESTS ON THE **UN-PROVEN?**

WELL, EVEN OLD **EUCLID** HAS TO TAKE **SOMETHING** FOR GRANTED!

This moment marked a terrible disappointment.

...But ignited the rest of my life.

PRIDE OF BAGHDAD

Written by: Brian K. Vaughn • Art by: Niko Henrichon • Published by: Vertigo; 2008

> "WAR ... WAR NEVER CHANGES."
> —NARRATOR, FALLOUT VIDEO GAME SERIES

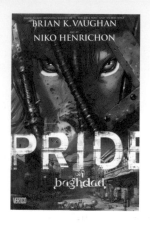

Ron Perlman's omen-infused voice doesn't lie; war *never* changes. Even if it's for a good reason (although both sides usually think it's for a good reason), there's still incalculable, unpredictable loss. In *Pride of Baghdad*, we see the uncertainty of war through the eyes of four lions, newly freed from the only home they've ever known—the zoo. [99]

Vaughn adds complexity to a seemingly-straightforward tale of survival through the use of these non-human main characters. The lions' beastly personalities and philosophies are often at odds; their interactions are nuanced, slowly unfolding to reveal layered depths as the story moves forward. Zill, the male of the group, gets presented as practical and alternatingly heroic and afraid. Noor, the matriarch of the pride, is honor-bound and

Nature and warfare collide.

---

99 Inspired by the real story of four lions who escaped the Baghdad zoo when the United States military bombed the city in 2003.

Noor curses having a life so out of her own control.

straightforward. Elder Safa's a grizzled, one-eyed badass who seems almost nihilistic in her survival philosophies, yet she readily puts herself in harm's way to protect her

pride. Lastly, Ali, the cub, is simple and cute, harkening back to *The Lion King*'s Simba—only Simba never had to deal with the harsh realities of war. Vaughn writes these lions with such wonderful subtleties that, by story's end, you'll find yourself turning the page slowly, hoping, *praying* for more time to get to know them.

As the lions try to survive in war-torn Baghdad, they encounter other animals, each of whom gives a unique viewpoint into their situation. Many of the animals feel unfettered thanks to the chaos, choosing to take and destroy in hollow re-enactments of their natural inclinations. A large turtle, with its impressive lifespan, tries to keep its head down and wait it out, uninterested in the reasons behind the humans' destruction, only in minimizing the inevitable losses behind it. Henrichon's art skillfully characterizes these disparate creatures without resorting to cartoonish exaggeration or minimalism. The few moments of beauty amidst the chaos are lushly illustrated, providing sharp contrast to the rebar, flames, and concrete of the bombed-out Baghdad.

War destroys. *Pride of Baghdad* anthropomorphizes Baghdad's animal population to provide multiple perspectives and philosophies on the horrors of warfare, ultimately showing that, no matter how righteous a cause is, there's always a cost to war, and it's often the most unexpected costs which are the most devastating.

LOST & FOUND

Written by/art by: Shaun Tan • The Rabbits written by: John Marsden • Published by: Arthur A. Levine Books; 2011

Some graphic novelists are primarily wordsmiths, utilizing simple imaging techniques as a means of conveying complex thoughts. Others are more "artists" in the traditional sense, using story as a backdrop to evoke emotion through the creation and application of breathtaking imagery. With Shaun Tan, author of *Lost & Found* and *The Arrival*, we get the artistic skills of a master painter and the elegant thoughtfulness of a poet.

According to Tan, *Lost & Found* deals primarily with the relationship between people and places.[100] In each of its three stories, we get different perspectives on this central theme. In *The Red Tree,* a young girl battles depression, each page illustrating a gorgeous visual metaphor for her emotional turmoil. In a crowded city street, she's isolated and alone, with a bloated, otherworldly fish hovering above her, black ichor leaking from its eyes. On another page she's desperately trying to stay afloat in a tiny ship amidst the turbulent waters of an aquatic graveyard of ocean liners. In another she's an actor in a strange play, holding a puppet of herself while performing for an impassive audience, mirroring the melancholic feeling of "going through the motions" experienced by many with depression. Dreamlike monsters, oppressive architecture, alien landscapes

... Tan fills every page with unique images that instill a sense of isolation and sadness into the reader. A single red leaf hides itself on every page until the very end, where it blooms into a lush, crimson beacon of life, radiantly representing all those things which pull us up during our darkest hours. *The Red Tree* deals quietly with serious emotional issues, but ultimately does so with optimism.

Earth has a long history of pale-skinned humans showing up to make life more difficult for their more pigmented brethren; *The Rabbits* uses white rabbits as a metaphor for such imperialism. In it, rabbits arrive in a new land. While they aren't directly unkind to its original inhabitants, they are uncaring, and spread throughout their new home like a plague, usurping the aboriginal tribes and relegating them to increasingly small tracts of land.

Lost & Found presents a clearer, more up-close, narrative than the other two stories in this collection. Here a wandering young man comes across an odd, living machine, paid heed by no one, and helps it search for a home. After traversing the city, talking to apathetic friends and strangers alike, he eventually finds a secret place for lost things—filled with mechanical creatures like this one, each one a uniquely assembled collection of parts both recognizable and not. Despite the lack of facial expressions or typical body shapes to these

100 *Lost & Found*, Shaun Tan.

darkness

overcomes you

creatures, you can see the joy, the *life,* to them, in both their movements and their interactions with one another. Later, our hero continues to see similar lost things, but over time he sees them more infrequently, unwittingly becoming more conformist, more self-serving as he grows older.

Lost & Found deals with many topics— altruism, responsibility, bystander apathy, cynicism. Perhaps most salient of these topics is the loss of imagination; as many people get older, the optimism and creativity they felt fades away, replaced by a gray, banal existence devoted to mediocrity and adherence to social norms. In the 2008 film *Step Brothers,* slacker step-bros Will Ferrel and John C. Reilly receive a pep talk from their dad, who tells them of his childhood dream—becoming a dinosaur.

He details the hours he spent stomping around his neighborhood, snarling and slobbering, until his own father told him to grow up and put away such childish notions. Which he did, dutifully, always intending to do the "adult" thing first, then come back to what his passion was, to never forget who he really was. But he didn't and he regretted it, and told his sons, "Don't lose your dinosaur." *Lost & Found* advocates a similar sentiment—don't let mediocrity and adulthood dull that which makes you shine.

In all of these stories, Tan creates breathtaking architecture and landscapes to represent the themes within each. *The Red Tree's* buildings loom heavily. *Lost & Found's* endless forests of gaskets, concrete, and curling shapes create Steampunk-esque structures which inspire feelings of conformity and hidden

The rabbits arrive.

liveliness. The titular Rabbits have massive ships and equipment all styled after the creatures themselves. Never one to waste space on a page, Tan uses different, evocative borders in each story. *Lost & Found's* gutter between the panels is filled with notes and blueprints to reflect its bespectacled, erudite hero, *The Red Tree* has pale colors to enhance the gloom of each image, and *The Rabbits* forgoes panel borders entirely to create massive, spilling images of the imperialists sweeping across the land as they please.

ARCHIE MARRIES...

Written by: Michael Uslan • Art by: Stan Goldberg and Bob Smith • Published by: Harry N. Abrams; 2010

Betty or Veronica? It's a decades-old question for Archie Andrews, who has been caught in a near-*menage a trois* since before most of us were born. Will our plucky everyman end up with Betty, the wholesome, supportive girl next door, or Veronica, the rich, worldly, and narcissistic dream girl? In *Archie Marries...* audiences finally get their answer. And the answer is *parallel timelines*.

On the eve of his high school graduation, a trip down memory lane becomes a walk through memories not-yet-remembered when Archie finds himself tumbling through two different timelines. In one, he and Betty tie the knot. In another, he and Veronica have a go at it. Uslan pays tribute to Archie's lengthy history by exploring different elements to these three main characters and their sizeable cast of secondary character.

With the Archie Marries Betty timeline, we see an exploration of the concept "know thyself." Archie and Betty move to New York City for a while, taking in the culture and hectic pace of the big city, all while struggling to find steady, satisfying work. Ultimately, the duo finds New York too callous for their liking and ends up back in their home town of Riverdale to settle down and raise their family. Archie and Betty both end up teaching at their old high school, while the burger-obsessed Jughead buys a burger joint and the various other side characters get in touch with their true natures. Throughout this storyline, we see characters longing for the past, for easier times, and for the simple comforts of home, ultimately encapsulating much of what's so enticing about Betty as a character—as the quintessential "girl next door," she represents the peaceful simplicity of an unornamented existence.

In the Archie Marries Veronica timeline, we see

"SO THIS IS 'GROWING UP?' "
—ARCHIE ANDREWS, REDHEAD AND PROUD OWNER OF NUMEROUS FRECKLES AND ONE JALOPY

After sixty years in school, Archie finally graduates.

a focus on self-improvement. Archie, as the poor kid courting a rich girl, has constantly battled thoughts of inadequacy, and here we finally get to see him overcome these doubts. In this timeline, he and most of the Riverdale gang work to shed their old flaws; Archie becomes a confident businessman, Reggie learns to swallow his pride and ask for help, and Veronica sets aside her vanity to put those she loves first. Both timelines are written satisfyingly; no matter where any Archie fan falls on the Betty/Veronica divide, or which side character was their favorite, they get a fitting, sweet ending to a debate that's raged for nearly a century.

"We needed to show the consequences, the butterfly effect, not only on Archie, Betty, and Veronica, but the butterfly effect his marriage would have on everybody in Riverdale, family and friends, because in real life a marriage does just that: it impacts everybody's lives, not just the lives of the two spouses." -Michael Uslan[101]

---

101 *Archie Marries...* Michael Uslan, Stan Goldberg, and Bob Smith.

VACANCY

Written by/art by: Jen Lee • Published by: Nobrow Press; 2015

What will the animals do once we're gone? In *Vacancy*, they'll dress in hipster clothes and wax reverentially about the place that's the ultimate

test of an animal's mettle, the place which separates the domesticated from the wild, the place that could end your journey before it ever begins— the woods.

Vacancy's short and sweet, coming in at less than thirty pages, but in its brevity it brings us a trio of charming characters: a dog, a raccoon, and a deer, whose varied animal personalities carry this story from start to finish. The raccoon's a self-serving, coy rapscallion, and the deer's a peace-keeper. As you might expect, the dog is loyal to the humans, expecting them to return any minute, oblivious to the truth. Jen Lee's orange, pink, and pale skies and ruined backgrounds are never directly mentioned, but it's clear that the dog's humans (and humans in general) are probably never coming back.

After a few run-ins with predators in the woods, the trio decides to return to the safety of the dog's

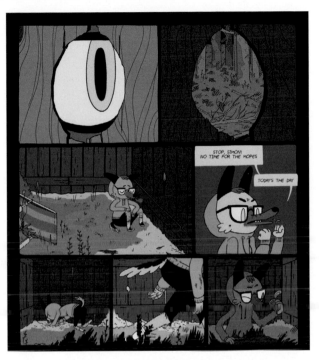

The dog just *knows* his owners will be back any moment.

backyard, opting for blind optimism in the face of darkness and danger. It's a quick, fun tale that puts the short in short story, but Lee's remarkable affinity for character voice and design make *Vacancy* an experience that lingers with you long after its brief runtime is over.

> "YOU GUYS GOING INTO THE WOODS?" –A DOG
> "KINDA, I GUESS." –A RACCOON

PALOMAR: THE HEARTBREAK SOUP STORIES

Written by/art by: Gilbert Hernandez • Published by: Fantagraphics; 2003

Gilbert Hernandez centers *Palomar: The Heartbreak Soup Stories* around a fictional Latin American town named Palomar, depicting the everyday lives of

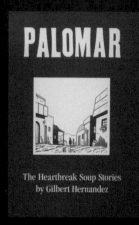

PALOMAR

The Heartbreak Soup Stories
by Gilbert Hernandez

the citizens in this small 'burg where technology seems to have derailed decades ago.

Palomar's narrative is an erratic hummingbird, flitting from character to character to character, rarely staying put for long or returning to the same place twice. One of the few frequently recurring characters is Luba, a newcomer to Palomar introduced as a banadora, "she who bathes others." Twenty years of her life are chronicled in Palomar, giving readers an in-depth investment in her story and the stories unfolding around her. Hernandez created a diverse cast of characters to populate this town, yet ties them all together with a focus on Latino culture. Hernandez

Hernandez often uses moving panels to intertwine multiple storylines.

remarked, "My goal is to tell stories that are engaging and entertaining for a general audience–but specifically to humanize Latinos, to give a different angle on Latinos from what is normally given in pop culture."[102]

Hernandez possess a unique talent in expressing complicated incidents in a panel or two, and in leaping around in time and place without knocking readers off-balance. During Palomar's whopping 520 pages, Hernandez shifts the tone significantly, covering light plotlines like a children's play to grim events such as a lurking serial killer. Hernandez sculpts explicit scenes of sexual escapades and violence,[103] keeping emotional resonance at the forefront through his use of powerful facial expressions and "old-school" artistic techniques.[104]

Hernandez's detailed art, intricate storytelling, and knack for eccentricity have cultivated the epic Palomar into a work well-worth investing the lengthy time into.

---

102 Quote retrieved from: https://www.guernicamag.com/daily/gilbert-hernandez-i-saw-my-neighborhood-as-the-world/.

103 Not in the same panel, of course.

104 Hernandez attributes his stylings as being a natural effect of his comparatively archaic toolset, saying he uses "Just pen and ink. It starts out with a piece of paper, a pencil, and an eraser. That's it."

WE3

Written by: Grant Morrison • Art by: Frank Quitely
Published by: Vertigo; 2004

Animals as test subjects are seen as an unfortunately crucial element to science. Heroic animals such as Laika give their lives in the name of progress, and while their sacrifices help save lives, there's always that larger, moral question underlying such research: If these animals had the power and awareness to choose their own fates, would they choose this? In WE3, we see that the answer is a resounding no.

Bandit, Tinker, and Pirate, otherwise known as 1, 2, and 3, are the subjects of a secret government experiment to turn animals into cybernetic military weapons. When the trio is about to be decommissioned in favor of less ... unsavory projects, their guilt-ridden caretaker gives them a chance at freedom, and they pounce on it.

WE3 is hard to read, not just for the graphic depictions of violence, but also for the pitiable plight of the titular trio. The three of them murder and maim with brutal efficiency, both under the service of the military and in trying to find their own freedom. Quitely uses boldly original art choices in depicting these action sequences, often using pseudo-three-dimensional panel layouts to convey altered perceptions of time. Morrison referred to the violence as a necessary part of the story, stating that it would "counterbalance the sentimentality that's always hard to avoid in tales of plucky animal pals."[105]

Morrison's writing and Quitely's art unite to depict the WE3, crafting them into deadly, sympathetic figures. They may be heavily-armed four-legged cyborgs in armored shells, but sticking out of those shells are three very fuzzy, very living faces of animals who just want to do anything other than kill people. The WE3 speak in stunted, broken English, rarely using more than two or three words at a time, conveying depth of character and stirring emotional reactions in the reader; had they spoken in complete sentences, they would have run the risk of seeming either cloying or immoral. Between each chapter is a handmade "Missing Pet" sign for the trio, pulling the heartstrings further when you realize that these poor animals weren't born and bred as weapons or test subjects, they were someone's friends. Like *Laika* after it, *WE3* calls into question the necessity of animal testing; its themes of rising military power and human detachment have become increasingly relevant in the United States as the government continues to increase its military force through the use of drones and other similar future tech.

Three faces down the newer model of killing machine.

105 *WE3*, Grant Morrison and Frank Quitely.

Quitely frequently uses non-traditional panel layouts to convey mass amounts of information with minimal space.

FRED THE CLOWN

Written by/art by: Roger Langridge • Published by: Fantagraphics; 2004

Fred the Clown is *damn* weird. It's also a smart parody of traditional comics and early film (among other things), but *man* is it strange.

"Was Fred the Clown real?" you'll wonder as you read through his fictional (?) history. "A lot of these comics aren't really ... funny. Not ha-ha funny, anyway," you'll muse after reading one of Fred the Clown's bleak adventures. "What's the deal with these fake ads? *Are* they fake?" you'll think as you browse page after page of comics and advertisements.

Of course, a cursory internet search will give (some) closure to your questions, but it won't change the experience of thumbing through page after page of comics, basking in Fred's misery as he fruitlessly pursues every woman he crosses paths with while trying to get his floundering comedy career to take off. *Fred the Clown*'s comics often end with non-canonical, nonsensical panels like Fred taking off his face to reveal a normal man underneath, only to take *that* face off to reveal a second Fred the Clown face. It's tonally ambiguous, intelligently absurd, and intricately constructed. Definitely not for the casual or undiscerning reader, but for anyone craving something subversive, something *weird, Fred the Clown* is like a fresh, delicious pie to the face.

Just one of Fred the Clown's many escapades.

"I HATE YOU."
—SIGNED,
FRED'S
VENTRILOQUIST
DUMMY

LAIKA

Written by/art by: Nick Abadzis • Published by: First Second; 2007

For decades, the United States and Soviet Union fought a war that was the national equivalent of catty high schoolers *Mean Girls*-ing each other behind their backs—most of the conflicts were indirect (but their presence felt), with each nation always competing against the other, watching out of the corner of their eye, trying to prove their superiority. Nowhere did this competition become as public as it did with the space race. While the United States was ultimately the first to put a human being on the moon, the Soviet Union launched the first unmanned satellite into space. Then they launched the first manned satellite into space, only in this case, the man was a dog.

Laika blends fact and fiction to bring the tale of Kudryavka, otherwise known as Laika, the first dog in space. *Laika* bounces around in time to paint the portrait of paranoia and fear permeating the Soviet Union in the mid-twentieth century, showing the quiet desperation of humans and canines alike as they struggled to eke out a meaningful existence. Laika's a brave, lovable pooch who endures a hard life; she's harangued, abandoned, and suffers constant hardship. Even Laika's happy moments are tinged with sadness as both her human caregivers and the reader know the inevitable is coming: For all her training, for all scientists' preparations, in their race for Soviet space superiority, the one contingency there wasn't time to plan for was to bring Laika home

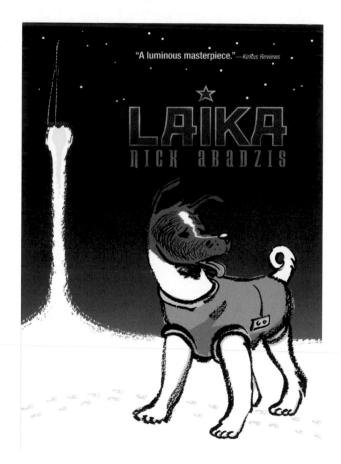

"A luminous masterpiece." —*Kirkus Reviews*

alive. Abadzis' ability to uncloyingly humanize this non-human hero against the backdrop of historical fiction makes *Laika* a heart-wrenching work sure to crack even the stoniest of hearts.

"WORK WITH ANIMALS IS A SOURCE OF SUFFERING TO ALL OF US. WE TREAT THEM LIKE BABIES WHO CANNOT SPEAK. THE MORE TIME PASSES, THE MORE I'M SORRY ABOUT IT. WE SHOULDN'T HAVE DONE IT ... WE DID NOT LEARN ENOUGH FROM THIS MISSION TO JUSTIFY THE DEATH OF THE DOG."
—OLEG GAZENKO, A RUSSIAN SCIENTIST AND GENERAL OFFICER IN THE SOVIET AIR FORCE

A brief moment of happiness for Laika.

UNDERSTANDING COMICS: THE INVISIBLE ART & MAKING COMICS: STORYTELLING SECRETS OF COMICS, MANGA AND GRAPHIC NOVELS

Written by/art by: Scott McCloud
Published by: William Morrow Paperbacks, 2004 (Understanding Comics); 2006 (Making Comics)

"UNDER THAT BROAD DEFINITION OF 'GRAPHIC NOVEL' THAT INCLUDES MEMOIR AND OTHER FORMS OF NONFICTION, UNDERSTANDING COMICS HAS TO BE ONE OF THE MOST SUCCESSFUL AND INFLUENTIAL GRAPHIC NOVELS. MOST OF THE COMICS SCHOLARSHIP IN THE 1990S CONSISTED OF EXTENDING OR REFUTING MCCLOUD'S IDEAS."[106]
–DR. RANDY DUNCAN, AUTHOR OF THE POWER OF COMICS: HISTORY, FORM AND CULTURE AND CREATING COMICS AS JOURNALISM, MEMOIR AND NONFICTION

Comics artist and scholar Scott McCloud took upon himself the Herculean task of analyzing the often-overlooked medium of comics. In *Understanding Comics,* McCloud depicts himself moving through the history and dimensions of comics, showing readers where comics began, the language they use, and their importance. From its first page, *Understanding Comics* is eagerly scholarly, reverent, thoughtful, and yet remarkably easy to pick up and read. McCloud covers a bevy of topics throughout the work, covering the vocabulary of comics with terms such as the icon,[107] the gutter,[108] and the panel transition,[109] a look into the importance of the line, a discussion of different comic styles around the globe, and much, *much* more. *Understanding Comics* is jam-packed with

---

107 Any image used to represent a person, place, thing, or idea. So, pictures qualify as icons as much as words do, meaning that the word icon is, itself, an icon, as are the words describing the iconography of the icon, furthermore ... (wanders off rambling).

108 The space between panels.

109 The method and meaning of the sequencing of panels on a page; McCloud described there as being six primary panel transitions. What are they? Why don't you read *Understanding Comics* and find out!

---

106 Quote retrieved from personal correspondence.

information, and McCloud's skill as both writer and artist allow him to convey this information with a smooth clarity. Fans of the comics genre, literary types, artists ... basically, any and everyone should read *Understanding Comics* to further their own understanding of this historic, ever-evolving art form.

Making Comics

Making Comics takes a slightly different approach to comics analysis than *Understanding*, aiming to act more as a guide for aspiring comics creators specifically rather than as a tool for greater blanket insight. In *Making Comics*, McCloud, still using a cartoonified symbol of himself as narrator (although this time with a bit of gray around his temples) provides salient lessons and examples for comics makers to learn from and grow.

While not quite as groundbreaking or approachable as *Understanding Comics, Making Comics* still provides an invaluable stroll through the art form well worth treading.

"THE POTENTIAL OF COMICS IS LIMITLESS AND EXCITING!"
–SCOTT MCCLOUD, UNDERSTANDING COMICS

Graphic Novels and Comics: The Visible Art

As we've gone through the countless graphic novels included in this book (and countless more deemed too rare or unworthy to include), a few things struck us. First, in putting this book together we tried to represent a wide variety of types of graphic novels, from the esoteric and weird to the heart-wrenching to the upbeat and youthful. Obviously not every great graphic novel could be included because we're only human[110] and there are only so many pages in a book, so consider this a starting point for you to use on your quest to conduct your own exploration.

Secondly, sweet *Petunia* do graphic novelists like showing graphic sex and nudity. From an artistic perspective it can be argued that the relative freedom of the medium allows artists to depict things as they want to without having a short-sighted higher-up censoring their work. It can also be argued that, sometimes, people just want to arbitrarily throw in some boobs and booties.

Third, we were awestruck by the sheer variety of content in graphic novels. Films, episodic series, video games, and other forms of popular media tend to play it relatively safe with the type of stories being told, and the result is often predictable, tiresome entertainment lacking much in the way of intellectual stimulation or actual entertainment value. Graphic novels, on the other hand, are fearless explorers of the edge, eager to bring forth the truth in any shape. In other mediums you'll be hard-pressed to locate stories as inventively weird as *The Frank Book,* as forthcoming and erudite as *Fun Home*, as brutally heartfelt as *Barefoot Gen,* or as personal as *Marbles.* They're out there, sure, but graphic novels are still the exemplary leaders in forging works of unique honesty. Every year more graphic novels are hitting shelves than the last, and with the ongoing popularity of comic book movies, webcomics, and an increasing awareness of comics in general, this growing trend will probably keep growing until it's unstoppable.

So! Whether you love to walk along the razor's edge with the iconoclasts, go white-knuckle with kinetic adventures, mull over life's most contemplative quandaries with memoirs and history, or voraciously read everything else in between, you can rest easy knowing that graphic novels have a long and lustrous past eager for you to explore it, and a magnificent future lying ever-onward.

—Katrina Hill and Alex Langley

---

110 As far as you know.

COMIC BOOK REFERENCES

Action Comics # 1 (1938). "Action Comics." Script: Jerry Siegel and Fred Guardineer, Art: Fred Guardineer and Bernard Baily and Joe Shuster.

All-Star Comics #8 (1941). "Introducing Wonder Woman." Script: William Moulton Marston, Art: Harry G. Peter.

Amazing Fantasy #15 (1962). "Introducing Spider-Man." Script by: Stan Lee, Art by: Steve Ditko.

Captain America Comics # 1 (1941). "Captain America Comics." Script: Joe Simon and Jack Kirby, Art: Jack Kirby.

Classic Comics #13 (1943) "Dr. Jekyll and Mr. Hyde." Script by: Robert Louis Stevenson, Art by: Arnold Hicks.

Detective Comics # 27 (1939). "The Case of the Criminal Syndicate." Script by: Bill Finger and Bob Kane, Art by: Bob Kane.

REFERENCES

About Faith. (2011). Retrieved from http://www.faitherinhicks.com/about/

An Interview with Howard Zinn. (n.d.). Retrieved from http://flag.blackened.net/ias/13zinn.htm

Anaïs Nin. (n.d.). Retrieved from https://en.wikiquote.org/wiki/Anaïs_Nin

Asano, I. (2013). *Solanin*. Hamburg: Tokyopop.

Beaton, K. (2013). "15th Century Peasant Romance Comics." Quote from http://www.harkavagrant.com/index.php?id=255

Bechdel Test Movie List. (n.d.). Retrieved from http://bechdeltest.com/statistics/

Bell, G. (2012). *The Voyeurs*. Minneapolis, MN: Uncivilized Books.

'Boxers & Saints' & Compassion: Questions For Gene Luen Yang. (n.d.). Retrieved from http://www.npr.org/2013/10/22/234824741/boxers-saints-compassion-quesions-for-gene-luen-yang

Bryan Lee O'Malley. (2007). Retrieved from http://www.avclub.com/article/bryan-lee-omalley-14171

Clance, P.R.; Imes, S.A. (1978). "The imposter

phenomenon in high achieving women: dynamics and therapeutic intervention." *Psychotherapy: Theory, Research and Practice* 15 (3): 241–247

Cooke, J. B., Staros, C., & Warnock, B. (2005). *Comic Book Artist*. Marietta, GA: Top Shelf Productions.

D. (2012). *My Driend Dahmer: A graphic novel*. New York: Abrams ComicArts.

'Doctor Strange And Doctor Doom: Triumph And Torment' Review. (n.d.). Retrieved from http://comicsalliance.com/doctor-strange-doctor-doom-triumph-and-torment-review-marvel/

Drawing From Life and Death. (2015). Retrieved March 13, 2016, from https://www.guernicamag.com/interviews/drawing-from-life-and-death/

Eisner, W. (2006). *The Contract with God Trilogy: Life on Dropsie Avenue*. New York: Norton

Eisner, W., & Buckley, P. (2008). *To the Heart of the Storm*. New York: Norton.

Fevers and mirrors: The surreal graphic novels of Charles Burns. (n.d.). Retrieved March from http://www.newstatesman.com/books/2014/10/fevers-and-mirrors-surreal-graphic-novels-charles-burns

Former Governor, Now Purdue President, Wanted Howard Zinn Banned in Schools. (n.d.). Retrieved from http://www.thewire.com/national/2013/07/former-ind-gov-daniels-now-purdue-president-wanted-howard-zinn-banned-schools/67256/

Frank Miller's 'Dark Knight' brought Batman back to life. (n.d.). Retrieved from http://www.nydailynews.com/entertainment/tv-movies/frank-miller-dark-knight-brought-batman-back-life-article-1.351685

Gilbert Hernandez: I Saw My Neighborhood as the World. (2015). Retrieved from https://www.guernicamag.com/daily/gilbert-hernandez-i-saw-my-neighborhood-as-the-world/

Gilchrist, T. (n.d.). '300: Rise of An Empire' Review: More of the Same, But Slightly Less. Retrieved from http://www.thewrap.com/300-rise-empire-review/

Gopalan, N. (July 16, 2008). "Alan Moore Still Knows the Score!" *Entertainment Weekly*

Gravett, P. (2005). *Graphic Novels: Everything You Need to Know*. New York: Collins Design.

Hayden, J., (2015). *The Story of My Tits*. New York: IDW.

Heater, B. (2006) *A Book Called Malice*, New York: New York Press.

How one man's lies almost destroyed the comics industry. (n.d.). Retrieved March 13, 2016, from http://io9.gizmodo.com/5985199/how-one-mans-lies-almost-destroyed-the-comics-industry

Inheritance. (n.d.). Retrieved from http://www.pbs.org/pov/inheritance/photo-gallery-art-spiegelman-maus/

Interview: Bryan Lee O'Malley (n.d.). Retrieved from http://manga.about.com/od/mangaartistinterviews/a/Interview-Bryan-Lee-O-Amalley.htm

Jennifer Hayden Tells 'The Story of My Tits' (n.d.). Retrieved from http://www.publishersweekly.

com/pw/by-topic/industry-news/comics/article/68648-jennifer-hayden-tells-the-story-of-my-tits.html

Jensen, J. (October 25, 2005). "Watchmen: An Oral History." Entertainment Weekly.

John Lewis Calls March On Washington 50 Years Ago 'One of This Nation's Finest Hours' (2013). Retrieved from http://abcnews.go.com/blogs/politics/2013/08/john-lewis-calls-march-on-washington-50-years-ago-one-of-this-nations-finest-hours/

Jordan, M. (n.d.). An Interview with Shaun Tan. Retrieved from http://www.bookslut.com/features/2009_07_014748.php

Kaplan, A. (2008). From Krakow to Krypton: Jews and comic books. Philadelphia: Jewish Publication Society.

Kirby, J., & Morrow, J. (2004). The Jack Kirby collector. Raleigh, NC: TwoMorrows.

Lerner, M. J., & Miller, D. T. (1978). Just world research and the attribution process: Looking back and ahead. Psychological Bulletin, 85(5), 1030–1051

Lewis, J., Aydin, A., & Powell, N. (2013). March.

McCloud, S. (1994). Understanding comics: the Invisible Art. New York: HarperPerennial.

McKay, A. (2008). Step-Brothers

Miller, F., & Mazzucchelli, D. (2005). Batman: Year One. New York: DC Comics.

Moore, A., & Lloyd, D. (2005). V for Vendetta. "Behind the Painted Smile." New York: Vertigo/DC Comics.

Morrison, G., & Quitely, F. (2005). WE3. New York: DC Comics.

Mullins, K. "Questioning Comics: Women and Autocritique in Seth's It's A Good Life, If You Don't Weaken." Canadian Literature, (203), 11–27.

Ms. Marvel': G. Willow Wilson, Sana Amanat on Kamala's transformation. Retrieved from http://herocomplex.latimes.com/comics/ms-marvel-g-willow-wilson-sana-amanat-on-kamalas-transformation/

Nate Powell on Swallow Me Whole, Mental Illness & the Magic of Siblings. (n.d.). Retrieved from http://blog.tfaw.com/2010/08/25/nate-powell-on-swallow-me-whole-mental-illness-the-magic-of-siblings/

Randle, C. (n.d.). Bryan Lee O'Malley Returns With His First New Comic Since Scott Pilgrim. Retrieved from http://www.slate.com/articles/arts/books/2014/07/interview_with_scott_pilgrim_writer_bryan_lee_o_malley_about_his_new_graphic.html

Randle, C. (2015). Jillian Tamaki: 'I need to spend less time in the minds of straight men' Retrieved from http://www.theguardian.com/books/2015/apr/24/jillian-tamaki-comics-graphic-novel-supermutant-magic-academy

Reinventing the pencil: 21 artists who changed mainstream comics (for better or worse). (2009). Retrieved from http://www.avclub.com/article/reinventing-the-pencil-21-artists-who-changed-main-30528

Schulz, L. C. (2010). The Dutch Hunger Winter and the developmental origins of health and disease. *Proceedings of the National Academy of Sciences, 107*(39), 16757-16758.

Scott McCloud Goes In-Depth On 'The Sculptor' [Interview]. (n.d.). Retrieved from http://comicsalliance.com/research-references-and-structuring-stories-scott-mccloud-goes-in-depth-on-the-sculptor-interview/

SDCC '15 Interview: Mariko Tamaki talks about. (2015). Retrieved from http://www.comicsbeat.com/sdcc-15-interview-mariko-tamaki-talks-about-this-one-summer/

Shared - Movies - Interviews - M - Moore Alan 060315. (n.d.). Retrieved from http://www.mtv.com/shared/movies/interviews/m/moore_alan_060315/

Sin City Movie Review & Film Summary (2005) | Roger Ebert. (n.d.). Retrieved from http://www.rogerebert.com/reviews/sin-city-2005

F.A.Q. | Tamaki, J. (n.d.). Retrieved from http://jilliantamaki.com/faq/

Tan, S., & Marsden, J. (2011). *Lost & found*. New York: Arthur A. Levine Books.

The Believer - Interview with Adrian Tomine. (2007). Retrieved March 14, 2016, from http://www.believermag.com/issues/200710/?read=interview_tomine

The Comics Reporter. (n.d.). Retrieved from http://www.comicsreporter.com/index.php/cr_sunday_interview_faith_erin_hicks/]

The Realest Comic About Growing Up Asian American, And Hating Yourself. (n.d.). Retrieved from http://kotaku.com/the-realest-comic-about-growing-up-asian-american-and-1724281672

Uslan, M., Goldberg, S., & Smith, B. (2010). *Archie Marries...* New York: Abrams ComicArts.

Walter Benjamin. (n.d.). Retrieved from https://www.goodreads.com/quotes/97949-history-is-written-by-the-victors

Wanzo, R. (2009). The Superhero: Meditations on Surveillance, Salvation, and Desire. *Communication and Critical/Cultural Studies, 6*(1), 93-97.

Watchmen's Legacy | The Paley Center for Media. (n.d.). Retrieved from http://www.paleycenter.org/watchmen-watchmens-legacy/

Wertham, F. (1954). *Seduction of the innocent*. New York: Rinehart.

Woodring, J. (2003). *The Frank Book*. Seattle, WA: Fantagraphics.

Wroe, N. (2004). Profile: Raymond Briggs. Retrieved from http://www.theguardian.com/books/2004/dec/18/featuresreviews.guardianreview8

Yang, B. (2010). *Forget sorrow: An ancestral tale*. New York: W.W. Norton.

COPYRIGHT CREDITS

Copyright credits for the graphic novels reviewed in this book are listed below by their page number in each chapter. Information was taken, when possible, from the copyright information that appears on the material as it originally appeared. When it was not possible, copyright information has been culled from reference materials. In no case does Krause Publications/F&W Media, Inc., claim ownership of the copyright to the material shown in the book.

Introduction
P. 6: © 1973, 1980, 1981, 1982, 1983, 1984, 1985, 1986 Art Spiegelman.

Chapter 1
P. 12: © 1938 Detective Comics, Inc. Image courtesy of Heritage Auctions.

P. 13: © 1962 Marvel Comics. Image courtesy of Heritage Auctions.

P. 14 and 15: © 2005 DC Comics.

P. 16 and 17: © 1989 Marvel Comics.

P. 18 and 19: © 1982 Marvel Comics.

P. 20: © 2004-2008 Marvel Comics.

P. 21: © 2008, 2009 and 2014 Marvel Comics.

P. 22: © 2015 DC Comics.

P. 23: © 2015 Marvel Comics.

P. 24 and 25: Cover, introduction and compilation © 2002 DC Comics. Originally published in single magazine form as *BATMAN: THE DARK KNIGHT RETURNS* 1-4. © 1986 DC Comics. Image courtesy of Heritage Auctions.

P. 26 and 27: Text and illustrations © 2013 Faith Erin Hicks.

P. 28 and 29: Originally published in single magazine form as *KINGDOM COME* 1-4 © 1996 DC Comics.

P. 30: © 2008 Alex Ross. Image courtesy of Heritage Auctions.

P. 31: Originally published in single magazine form by DC Comics/Wildstorm as *EX MACHINA* 1-5 © 2004 Brian K Vaughan and Tony Harris.

P. 32 and 33: © 1988, 1989 DC Comics. Cover and compilation © 1990 DC Comics. Introductions © 1988, 1990 DC Comics.

P. 34, 35 and 36: Cover and compilation © 1986, 1987 DC Comics. Originally published in single magazine form as *WATCHMEN* 1-12. © 1986, 1987 DC Comics.

P. 37, 38 and 39: Cover, introduction, afterword and compilation © 2008 DC Comics. Originally published in *BATMAN: THE KILLING JOKE, BATMAN BLACK AND WHITE* 4. © 1988, 1996 DC Comics.

P. 40: © 20th Century Fox. Image courtesy of Heritage Auctions.

P. 41: Clockwise from top: © Warner Bros. Pictures; © Legendary Pictures/DC

Comics/Warner Bros. Pictures/
Paramount Pictures; © Village
Roadshow Pictures/Vertigo/
Warner Bros. Pictures. All
images courtesy of Heritage
Auctions.

P. 42: © Dark Castle Entertainment/
Warner Bros. Pictures. Image
courtesy of Heritage Auctions.

P. 43: © 20th Century Fox. Image
courtesy of Heritage Auctions.

Chapter 2

P. 44: © Junji Ito/Shogakukan Inc./
Viz Media.

P. 45: © 1943 Gilberton Co. Image
courtesy Heritage Auctions.

P. 48 and 49: © 2005 Charles Burns.

P. 50 and 51: Text © 2010 Susan
Kim and Laurence Klavan.
Illustrations © 2010 Faith Erin
Hicks.

P. 52 and 53: Story © 2011
Steve Niles, art © 2011 Ben
Templesmith, © 2011 Idea and
Design Works, LLC.

P. 54 and 55: © Junji Ito/
Shogakukan Inc./Viz Media.

P. 56: © 2015 Junji Ito/Viz Media.

P. 57: © 2006 Shaun Tan.

P. 58 and 59: © 2014 Margaret K.

McElderberry Books.

P. 60 and 61: © Severed Comics
LLC.

P. 62 and 63: © 2002 Junji Ito/
Shogakukan Inc.

Chapter 3

P. 64: © 2015 Jillian Tamaki.

P. 66 and 67: Name, text and art ©
2015 Alex Langley.

P. 68, 69 and 70: © 2014, 2015
Marvel Comics.

P. 71 and 72: © 2010 Raina
Telgemeier.

P. 73 and 74: Text © 2008 Mariko
Tamaki. Illustrations © 2008
Jillian Tamaki.

P. 75 and 76: © 2015 Svetlana
Chmakova. Application
copyright © 2010 Hatchette
Book Group, Inc.

P. 77 and 78: © Bryan Lee
O'Malley/Oni Press.

P. 79 and 80: © 2006 Gene Yang.

P. 81 and 82: Text and illustrations
© 2012 Faith Erin Hicks.

P. 83: Text and illustrations © 2013
Faith Erin Hicks.

P. 84 and 85: © 2015 Victoria
Jamieson.

P. 86 and 87: Story © 2014 Cory

Doctorow. Art and adaptation
© 2014 Jen Wang.

P. 88 and 89: © 2008 Inio Asano/
Viz Media LLC.

P. 90 and 91: © 2003 Craig
Thompson/Top Shelf.

P. 92 and 93: © 2012 Raina
Telgemeier.

P. 94 and 95: Text © 2014 Mariko
Tamaki. Art © 2014 Jillian
Tamaki.

P. 96 and 97: © 2011 Vera Brosgol.

P. 98 and 99: © 2015 Jillian Tamaki.

Chapter 4

P. 100: Volume I © 1973, 1980,
1981, 1982, 1983, 1984, 1985,
1986 Art Spiegelman. Volume
II © 1986, 1989, 1990, 1991 Art
Spiegelman.

P. 102 and 103: © 1987 Keji
Nakazawa. Translation
copyright © 1987 Project
Gen. Introduction © 1990 Art
Spiegelman.

P. 104 and 105: © 2013 John Lewis/
Andrew Aydin/Nate Powell/
Top Shelf Productions.

P. 107 and 108: Text and
illustrations © 2012 John
Backderf.

P. 109: © 2006 Cat Dancer Corporation and Dan E. Burr.

P. 110: From the top: © 2006 Cat Dancer Corporation and Dan E. Burr. © 2013 Cat Dancer Corporation and Dan E. Burr.

P. 111 and 112: Volume I © 1973, 1980, 1981, 1982, 1983, 1984, 1985, 1986 Art Spiegelman. Volume II © 1986, 1989, 1990, 1991 Art Spiegelman.

P. 113 and 114: © 2010 Belle Yang.

P. 115 and 116: © 1982 Raymond Briggs.

P. 118: © Marvel Studios/Walt Disney Studios. Image courtesy of Heritage Auctions.

P. 119: From left: © Good Machine/Dark Horse Entertainment/Fine Line features/HBO Films. © Tokyo Movie Shinsha/Toho. Images courtesy Heritage Auctions.

P. 120: © 2005 L'Association, Paris, France.

P. 121: © 2012 Leela Corman

P. 122 and 123: © 2009 David Small.

P. 125 and 125: © 2006 The Estate of Will Eisner. *A Contract with God* © 1978, 1985, 1989, 1995 Will Eisner. *A Life Force* © 1983, 1984, 1985, 1988, 1995 Will Eisner. *Dropsie Avenue: The Neighborhood* © 1995 Will Eisner.

P. 126 and 127: © 1995 Howard Cruse/Paradox Press. © 2010 Howard Cruse/Vertigo.

P. 128 and 129: The material in this collection first appeared in *Palestine* #1-9 © 1993, 1994, 1995, 1996, 2001 Joe Sacco.

P. 130 and 131: Text © 2012 Mark Long and Jim Demonakos. Illustrations © 2012 Nate Powell. Compilation © 2012 Mark Long, Jim Demonakos, and Nate Powell.

P. 132 and 133: © 2008 Howard Zinn, Mike Konopacki, and Paul Buhle.

P. 134 and 135: Translation copyright © 2003 L'Association, Paris, France.

P. 136 and 137: © 1991 Will Eisner.

P. 138 and 139: © 2013 Gene Luen Yang.

Chapter 5

P. 140: © 2006 Shaun Tan.

P. 142: Cover and compilation © 1991 DC Comics. Introduction © 1995 DC Comics. Originally published in single magazine form as The Sandman 1-8. © 1988, 1989 DC Comics.

P. 143 and 144: © 2015 Noelle Stevenson/HarperTeen.

P. 144 and 145: © 2010 Doug TenNapel.

P. 146 and 147: © 2014 Bryan Lee O'Malley.

P. 148 and 149: © Linda Medley. Compilation © 2006 Fantagraphic Books.

P. 150 and 151: Cover, text and compilation © 2011 Gabriel Bá and Fábio Moon. Originally published in single magazine form as *Daytripper* 1-10. © 2010 Gabriel Bá and Fábio Moon.

P. 152 and 153: © 2014 Brian K. Vaughan/Pia Guerra/Vertigo.

P. 154 and 155: Text and illustrations © 2010 Ben Hatke.

P. 156 and 157: © 2012 Jeff Lemire.

P. 158 and 159: © 2012 Mark Siegel.

P. 160 and 161: © 2015 Kate Beaton.

P. 162 and 163: © 2006 Shaun Tan.

Chapter 6

P. 164: © 2008 Nate Powell.

P. 166: © 1972 Justin Green/Last Gasp.

P. 167 and 168: © 2012 Ellen Forney.

P. 169 and 170: © 2006 Alison Bechdel.

P. 171 and 172: © 1993, 1994, 1995, 1996, 2003 Seth (G. Gallant).

P. 173 and 174: © 2001 Dylan Horrocks.

P. 174 and 175: © 2012 Glyn Dillon.

P. 176: Characters, stories, and art © 2004, 2005, 2006, 2007 Adrian Tomine.

P. 177 and 178: © 2001 Daniel Clowes/Pantheon/Jonathan Cape.

P. 179: © 2013 Rutu Modan.

P. 180 and 181: © 2008 Nate Powell.

P. 182: © 2011 Nate Powell.

P. 182 and 183: © 2003 Jeffrey Brown.

P. 184 and 185: © 2015 Jennifer Hayden.

P. 186 and 187: © 2009 Dave Mazzucchelli/Pantheon.

P. 188 and 189: ©2012 Gabrielle Bell.

P. 190 and 191: Text and art © 2015 Scott McCloud.

P. 192, 193 and 194: Characters, stories, and art © 2015 Adrian Tomine.

P. 195: Characters, stories, and art © 1998, 1999, 2000, 2001, 2002, 2003 Adrian Tomine.

Chapter 7

P. 196: © 2004, 2005, 2011, 2014 Grant Morrison and Frank Quitely.

P. 198 and 199: © 2003 Jim Woodring.

P. 200 and 201: © 2005 Seth.

P. 202 and 203: © 1993-present Chris Ware.

P. 204 and 205: © 2010, 2012 and 2014 Charles Burns.

P. 206 and 207: © 2009 Logicomix Print Ltd.

P. 208 and 209: © 2006 Brian K. Vaughan and Niko Henrichon.

P. 210, 211 and 212: *The Red Tree* © 2001 Shaun Tan. *The Lost Thing* © 2000 Shaun Tan. *The Rabbits*: text copyright © 1998 Jomden Pty Ltd; illustrations © 1998 Shaun Tan. Additional artwork copyright © 2011 Shaun Tan. Additional text copyright © 2011 Shaun Tan and Jomden Pty Ltd.

P. 213 and 214: © 2010 Archie Comic Publications, Inc.

P. 215: © 2015 Jen Lee/Nobrow.

P. 216: © 2003 Gilbert Hernandez/ Fantagraphics Books.

P. 218 and 219: © 2004, 2005, 2011, 2014 Grant Morrison and Frank Quitely.

P. 220 and 221: © 2004 Roger Langridge/Fantagraphics Books.

P. 222 and 223: © 2007 Nick Abadzis.

P. 224-226: © 2004, 2006 Scott McCloud/William Morrow Paperbacks.

INDEX